THE G
GOLDEN PATH

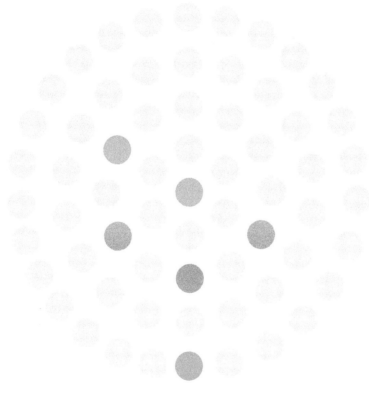

LOVE
A guide to your Venus Sequence

GENE KEYS

This edition published in Great Britain and USA 2020
by Gene Keys Publishing Ltd
13 Freeland Park, Wareham Road, Poole BH16 6FA

Richard Rudd

THE GENE KEYS GOLDEN PATH
LOVE
A guide to your Venus Sequence

Print edition ISBN 978-1-9996710-1-3
Kindle edition ISBN 978-1-8380487-1-6

genekeys.com

CONTENTS

ABOUT THE AUTHOR

Richard Rudd is an international teacher, writer and award-winning poet. His mystical journey began early in life when he experienced a life changing state of spiritual illumination over 3 days and nights in his twenties. This catalysed an extensive worldwide spiritual search. All his studies became synthesised in 2002 when he began to write and receive the Gene Keys – a vast synthesis exploring the miraculous possibilities inherent in human DNA. It took seven years to write the book as well as understand and embody its teachings. Today Richard continues to study and teach the profound lessons contained in the Gene Keys.

FOREWORD

To have bought this book, you must already be a person with more than just idle curiosity. You must be a sincere seeker after some significant inner light of some kind. If you are following the Golden Path Program you will by now have had an introduction to the Gene Keys, to your Hologenetic Profile and to the principles of the ancient I Ching and its patterns, lines and their application to your life. The Venus Sequence takes this further. It takes the journey much further.

I often feel a deep privilege to be the recipient of a wisdom like the Gene Keys. I hope that at the end of my life I will look back and feel a certain deep satisfaction that I was able to leave something of value behind for future generations. But standing above all else - the pinnacle - at least for me - has to be this body of wisdom called The Venus Sequence. It has transformed my life more than any other aspect of these teachings. It has brought me face-to-face with my deepest evolutionary 'edge'. It has also guided me like an old friend through some very tempestuous seas.

I look back to the man I was before I knew the meaning of my Venus Sequence. I was like a child in my relationships. There were vital lessons that no one had ever taught me - like how to take full responsibility for my feelings in the moment. Like the value of commitment and patience as the two great wings upon which unconditional love soars.

Now I am a new man. I am imperfect for sure, and probably more than most, but I have one thing going for me - I have learned how to love. I have learned the greatest art any human can ever learn - how to return non-love with love. This is the heart of the Venus Sequence.

I have a hunch about this wisdom. I think it is the beginning of a quiet revolution across our planet. A revolution in our relationships. I think it is going to help change the world, and I can only say such an outrageous and daring thing because it has so utterly changed my world. I therefore wish you well as you begin your journey into your Venus Sequence. My only advice is to tread softly and to travel if possible in company. The Venus Sequence thrives on support, on friendship and above all else, it thrives on love.

Richard Rudd

1. INTRODUCTION

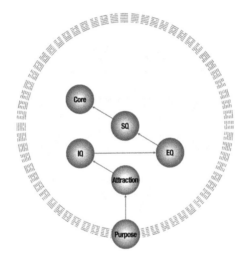

YOUR VENUS SEQUENCE
OPENING YOUR HEART

A HEARTFELT WELCOME

Welcome to the Venus Sequence. If you have come this far and given yourself enough time to digest your Activation Sequence, then you have proved to yourself that you are now ready to move into a deeper transformation. The Venus Sequence may well be one of the deepest transformation experiences you ever move through. When I first received the transmission of the Venus Sequence, it opened me up to something that seemed almost to be a dream – that is, the promise of a life lived with a consistently open heart.

Now I know that in the modern New Age movement, everyone always talks about living with an open heart. But what does that really involve? This is the question at the heart of the Venus Sequence. Can you keep your heart open under intense judgement? Can you find enough self-love to overcome harsh personal rejection? Are you able to forgive offences instantaneously? Are such things possible for you? In order for us to be able to live with an open heart, we will first of all have to remember what that feels like. It is unlikely to be a fast-track path, but it is the biggest adventure of a lifetime. Nothing in your outer life can compare to the depth of self-fulfilment that will come from achieving this extraordinary thing.

When you embark upon this next stage into your Venus Sequence, you must cultivate exceptional patience. The more you are able to be patient, the quicker the process will seem to move.

As you learn about the intricacies of your own emotional wounding, you are likely to come face to face with some harsh truths about yourself. You will therefore need to learn to be fiercely honest with yourself. It is also likely that you will go

3

through difficult phases in which you may feel as though you are not getting anywhere, so you will also need a large dose of perseverance.

These three qualities of patience, honesty, and perseverance will be vital allies for you in the weeks and months ahead. Above all however, you will need to learn the art of compassion – that elusive spring hidden in a secret glade somewhere deep inside your heart. Your compassion is paramount – the ability to parent yourself when wounded, to forgive yourself your perceived failures, and to look upon yourself with constant gentle wonder.

This is your charge as you enter your Venus Sequence. Please give yourself a heartfelt welcome.

ENTERING THE VENUS STREAM

Before we enter into the Venus Sequence, I would like to share a little about the actual experience I had in receiving this wisdom. It was a sunny summer afternoon, and I was flying quite high having just completed teaching a 3-day seminar on the Gene Keys. It was the first time I had publicly introduced the 3 levels of awareness now known as the Shadow, the Gift, and the Siddhi. The actual names for the 64 Siddhis had only come to me in the 2 days leading up to the course itself, so you might imagine how my mind was racing to keep up with this rapidly unfolding revelation.

I was sitting on the train on the way home, when all of a sudden I began to see a vast web of geometric patterns connecting up the 64 hexagrams of the I Ching. The patterns were intricate and vastly complex, but also beautiful like fractal patterns. I entered spontaneously into a heightened state of consciousness that lasted for the next 3 days. It was only afterwards that I learned that there had been a rare transit of the planet Venus across the face of the sun on that very day that I began seeing these patterns. It was in the following three days that I received the revelations of the Venus Sequence. There was a vast flood of insight moving behind the wisdom itself, and I saw many things that are now a silent part of my knowing, or are no longer accessible to my ordinary waking mind. Being so utterly subjective, revelations are difficult things to explain!

Central to this revelation is the energy, pathway, and positioning of the planet Venus. But it is also much more than just a celestial object; it is a stream of consciousness that happens to relate to Venus, perhaps in a holographic way, certainly in an archetypal way. I call this phenomenon 'the Venus Stream'. It is a living transmission of energy and wisdom. This idea of the Gene Keys as a living transmission is something I have shared in the past, but it is not an easy thing to explain to the left-brain mind. When I received this knowledge back in 2004, I had no real context to place it in. It was a pure revelation – so raw and potent that it drove me to the very edges of reason. I have spent many years since grappling with the weight of this wisdom.

Now, in the framework of the whole Golden Path, the Venus Sequence has a clear context. I have come to realise that it is not something to be entered into lightly. The Activation Sequence prepares you to enter the Venus Stream. But unlike your Activation Sequence, the Venus Sequence moves in a far more feminine and sinuous way. Insights will come from the right brain, from the heart of your intuition.

This means that your logic will have to catch up afterwards, after the actual transformations have occurred. So this is a wisdom that cannot be rushed. You can rush in with your mind, but if you aren't aligned with the Stream itself, then you will just have a mental journey. To enter into the Venus Stream is to allow yourself to be swept into an awesome process of deep and lasting transformation. The transmutation through the Venus Stream is an emotional one. Your emotions are the raw material of this journey. They provide the thrust that will allow you to navigate the twists and turns of your karma.

THE ALLEGORY OF WATER

The ancient Taoists often spoke of wisdom by relating it to water. They referred to the spiritual path of the true human being as the 'Watercourse Way'. As I have contemplated the Venus Sequence down the years, I have come to see the various pathways that comprise the Venus Sequence as reflecting the various different movements of water.

For example, the first Pathway of Dharma is like the movement of water deep under the ground. It moves through caves and underground waterfalls and reservoirs, and it only emerges into the light as the Pathway of Karma, which is like a spring bubbling up from under the ground. As you travel along the Pathways of the Venus Sequence, the Stream will guide your contemplation. There will be times where you are changing internally in ways that you cannot see, and times when revelations suddenly erupt and shake the parameters of your mind.

Your contemplative journey through the Venus Sequence therefore follows an allegorical watery thread, and once you have entered the Stream you can only surrender to the twists and turns of the transmission as it moves inside you. The Great Change that is spoken of in the Gene Keys book is a fundamental shift in human consciousness. This will come about as our emotional awareness reaches the pinnacle of its maturity, at which point our awareness becomes universal, riding on the refined waves of our old emotional life. We are entering a new world, moving across an epic threshold, and this new energy within us, this feminine Venus Stream - is propelling the shift.

THE GIFTS OF GRACE AND THE 22ND GENE KEY

As you will learn, the Venus Sequence is a journey right into the heart of human suffering. It shows you the mechanics of your individual suffering in the form of the string of Shadow patterns that you have inherited through your ancestral DNA. However, the Venus Sequence shows us much more than this. It also gives us a grand backdrop to the reason for suffering itself. By helping you to understand your own patterns as aspects of a greater collective theme, this wisdom points your awareness right at the heart of the issue – namely, our desire to escape the pain.

This very human trait of wanting to flee from pain is totally understandable. At a purely physical level, it is indeed a defence reflex inside us. However, there are deeper reasons for our pain than we usually realise. Few people have discovered the true secret of suffering – that it is a doorway to Grace. Our pain is always trying to tell us something important, and if we can summon the courage to lean into the pain and listen to its message, then we will always discover its hidden gift. Every Shadow contains a Gift. Nowhere is this truer than in your journey through the Venus Sequence.

When the Gene Keys book was first written, some of the Keys emerged in a very sketchy form, as though they were not yet ready to arrive. When I sat down to edit the work, I came across one Gene Key – the 22nd Gene Key – that seemed to be completely hidden from me.

As I read my first words on this Gene Key whose highest expression is Grace, I realised that I hadn't even touched its core, so I decided to completely delete what I had written, and wait for it to re-emerge. This didn't happen until almost a year later when I was emerging from a particularly bad winter illness. When the 22nd Gene Key did finally spill out into words, I was quite stunned. It stands alone in the book, almost like a book within the book. Although similar to the 55th Gene Key (its brother) in length, its content encompasses an extraordinary panorama of consciousness. At its heart however lies the question of human suffering, and it therefore has a direct relationship to the Venus Sequence. Both are manifestations of the Venus Stream. The more you read and digest the 22nd Gene Key, the more you will settle yourself into the Venus Stream.

OPENING YOUR HEART THROUGH RELATIONSHIPS

As we have seen, the Venus Stream involves the mystical role of Grace, and Grace is a force that comes from above. It is beyond our reckoning. It cannot be predicted or caused, only invited. When we say that Grace comes from above, we are not saying that it is outside us. It simply resides in a part of our greater self that currently lies outside our direct reach.

But we can invite Grace into our lives through facing into our own pain, through taking full responsibility for our Shadow patterns, and through deep self-compassion. The Venus Stream constantly reminds us to be gracious, towards ourselves and towards all beings.

As we learn to be gracious, we can learn once again to open our hearts fully to life, to all aspects of life, even the darker sides. This is where the Venus Stream will lead you, into the secret chambers of your own heart. Even when your heart feels completely closed, the Stream will wrap itself around you, and invite you to bring yourself back to life. Just as in the stories of old from all around the globe, we always have the capacity to resurrect ourselves from our own harshness. Who knows why things happen the way they happen? This is one of the great mysteries of the word Dharma, the first Pathway of the Venus Sequence. We can only surrender graciously to fate, and as we do so, we raise the frequency of our response to life. This is when Grace becomes possible – at the exact moment of our deepest surrender.

Because the Venus Stream leads us through the territory of our emotions, it cannot help but be a journey that is all about relationships. What would be the purpose of an open heart if not to relate with others? Here we touch the essence of life. When you ask those who are dying what in their lives has mattered to them the most, they will almost always tell you the names of their loved ones and friends. The Venus Sequence stands on the pillars of your 4 Prime Gifts, but it brings them into contact with others. It tests your capacity to embody your Gifts over and over again through the education of your relationships. And eventually, as you learn to stabilise your Gifts and stand in your Core Stability with your heart open, then you will witness the flowering of your life within the wider community through the Pearl Sequence.

The Venus Sequence is really where the coalface of this work with the Gene Keys is found. It may take you many years to plumb the depths of your Venus Sequence, so you will need those three qualities of patience, perseverance, and honesty every step of the way. But you don't have to rush at this work too intensely.

You may touch into it, and then withdraw for a period to let it settle deeper inside you. Then you can dive in again and get mining for those diamonds. You will have to find your own rhythm of working and playing with the Golden Path.

One thing is for certain; your relationships will keep reflecting back to you exactly how far your understanding is progressing. So please feel free to use this wisdom however you feel drawn to using it. If you feel to share it, then share it, if you need to keep it for yourself as an internal practise; that is also fine. There are no rules and no right way or wrong way. It is your journey, so you should follow your heart as you drift, dive, plummet, rise up, and immerse yourself in the living waters of the Venus Stream.

2. THE PATHWAY OF DHARMA

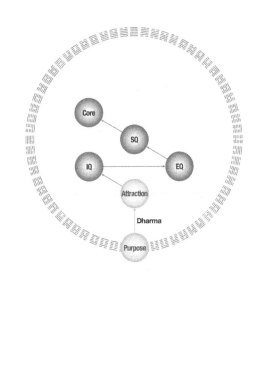

DHARMA

As you anchor yourself deeply into the Sphere of your Purpose, so you influence all aspects of your Hologenetic Profile. Your Purpose is like a biological nexus. It is the foundation stone of who you are. Out of the qualities of the Gene Key of your Purpose arise the manifestations of your life. Leading deeper into yourself, beyond the domain of your physical body, the Pathway of Dharma is a bridge to another plane of reality – a dimension sometimes known as the 'Astral Plane'. We will look more deeply into this area as we enter into the Sphere of Attraction, which lies at the other end of this Pathway of Dharma. For now, it is enough to understand that we humans have subtler layers to our being than our current reality attests.

THE PATHWAY OF DHARMA

Dharma is a wonderful word of many dimensions. The beauty of such a word is that it does not come pre-defined. Rather you can let it define itself within your understanding.

In ancient China around the time of the genesis of the I Ching, one of the most prevalent traditions was the natural philosophy of Taoism. Central to Taoism is the notion of the 'Tao', the natural harmonic 'way' or flow of life. Like the word Dharma, the Tao points towards a quality so subtle and pervasive that it cannot be put into words. It can only really be lived and embodied. The Pathway of your Dharma is really about your destiny. Along this Pathway flows the mysterious current of evolution and its counterpart, the current of involution. These are currents that flow deep beneath our conscious awareness. They may be captured through our resonance to myths or archetypes, or through poetry, music, or dreams.

From deep within the unconscious folds of an opium trance, the English poet Coleridge wrote the following famous lines:

In Xanadu did Kubla Khan
A stately pleasure-dome decree:
Where Alph, the sacred river, ran
In caverns measureless to man
Down to a sunless sea

These lines capture beautifully the archetypal essence of this Pathway of Dharma. They refer to a mythical garden, a kind of Eden, through which the sacred river of life flows. The garden might well be seen as our lives, and the pleasure-dome our physical body. But deep below the surface of our lives lie the mysterious currents of the unseen world. The sacred river is the path of our true destiny as it emerges from the void, that 'sunless sea', and passes through great underground caverns, the quantum dimensions below our conscious awareness. It is an apt allegory, the underground river, for it hints at the vast mystery of the inner life.

Perhaps the greatest turning point in a person's life is the realisation of the existence of the inner life. We are so often caught in the drama of our external lives that we neglect the greater part of our being. Like the iceberg, our true worth lies hidden beneath the surface.

Our intention, our unconscious attitude, and our deep sense of purpose all dictate the outer life. And to access the inner fabric of our reality we must turn within. Contemplation is such a turning inwards. This entire voyage along the Golden Path affords us an enrichment of our inner life.

FROM DRAMA TO DHARMA

The Venus Sequence provides each of us with a transformational map that opens an eye on the unconscious hidden forces that motivate all our relationships. It is a kind of relationship yoga. In the Taoist tradition of ancient China, disciples on the spiritual path were trained in two contrary but complementary approaches to spirituality. These were known as the 'Wai Dan' and 'Nei Dan' trainings. The Wai Dan way emphasised external techniques such as yoga, the martial arts, or strenuous physical exercise. Such techniques brought external strength, balance, and harmony in the outer life. Conversely, the Nei Dan way emphasised the cultivation of the subtle inner life using techniques such as meditation or contemplation.

As we enter the Venus Sequence, we will be looking at our relationships through both views – we will employ external techniques to enhance our awareness of Shadow patterns, particularly in intense emotional situations. And we will continue in our deeper contemplation of our Profile. As our awareness burrows into our lives on increasingly deeper levels, we may come across some of these deep caverns of insight as we touch the source of our Dharma.

Interestingly, to the Taoists, the ultimate inner training came about through a deep interior study of the dynamics of the I Ching. The codes within the text have a way of resonating to the hidden forces at work behind the present moment.

The Gene Keys transmission challenges you to find the living text within your DNA, without the need to consult an external means of advice. This is an intense spiritual work when you bring it into the domain of relationships, because there the external drama tends to be at its thickest.

Therefore we will use our relationships as our means of transformation. Wherever the drama is greatest for you, whether it's your husband, wife, parent, child, partner, enemy, or friend, there is the place of greatest potential and magic.

This work with the Gene Keys is a modern spiritual path in its own right. Most of us are no longer called to enter the monastic way in this day and age. We must find the transformation in our everyday lives. Deep contemplation on the way you behave in all your relationships will betray hidden patterns of resistance to your Dharma. These teachings are about letting go of your self-image. Where your Dharma is concerned, you can only surrender.

3. THE SPHERE OF YOUR PURPOSE

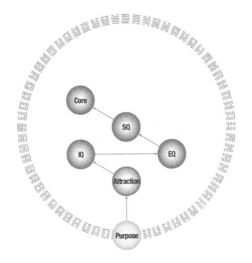

THE SPHERE OF YOUR PURPOSE IN RELATIONSHIPS

Now we will revisit the Sphere of your Purpose, as it lies at the foot of your Venus Sequence, but we will train our contemplation on it in another dimension. Every relationship in your life brings you the opportunity to find a deeper relationship to your own true purpose. This is a sentence to contemplate. In the modern age, when relationships become very difficult, no matter how hard we may try to save the relationship, many of us can find no other alternative but separation. However, when you really understand the core message of your Venus Sequence, you may reframe the whole purpose of the relationships in your life.

We tend to see the purpose of our relationships as a means to bring more happiness into our lives, and this is a worthwhile and very understandable sentiment. However, sometimes we need to go deeper into ourselves to find the diamonds. We need to consider where happiness comes from, and is it the same as fulfilment? We have seen through the Activation Sequence that our true Purpose is not an external thing. It is a quality of our consciousness. You are invited to look again at the Siddhi of the Gene Key of your Purpose. This is the purpose of your relationships – to exponentially enhance that quality in your life.

Ironically, it is when relationships become the most challenging that you have the greatest opportunity to transform the Shadow pattern that is preventing this quality from emerging in your life. If such a beautiful quality is dependent on any outer condition or person, then you cannot yet be deeply rooted in its field of emergence. I hope that this gives you pause for thought.

THE IMPORTANCE OF COMMITMENT

One of the great questions explored in relationships is the issue of commitment. It is easy to misunderstand the meaning of true commitment in our relationships. Our deepest commitment must always be to our own truth - this means that we need to be utterly honest with ourselves, and take responsibility for our own Shadow patterns.

Every relationship has its own karmic cycle, and in order to reap the greatest reward from the relationship, we need to honour it fully. Sometimes we bring an end to a relationship without giving it everything. It is not a failure if a relationship ends. All things have life cycles. But an ending may well be a lost opportunity.

There is no situation that cannot teach you to open your heart more. There is no relationship that cannot bring you to a deeper sense of your own true Purpose. Often the more intense the relationship, the more potential value it holds for you. The Venus Sequence may not be an easy path, but if it is deeply imbibed it may be one of the fastest paths towards Truth that the modern world can offer. Your commitment to your highest potential will be tested over and over again by your relationships. How deep does your commitment really go?

Despite the above, you need to know that the Venus Sequence has no moral agenda. Sometimes a relationship reaches a natural closure. You can always tell that the closure is a part of your Dharma, because the relationship ends with graciousness on both sides. The only exception to this is a physically abusive relationship. Such a situation requires professional guidance, and if you find yourself in such a position, you should seek counsel immediately.

Emotional abuse is a different matter from physical abuse. Emotional abuse can teach you an extraordinary gift, if you have the depth of commitment to your own heart.

Emotional abuse can teach you forgiveness. In fact, emotional abuse can teach you that there is no such thing as emotional abuse except through your own choice. We choose whether we are a victim of someone else's pattern or not. Therefore emotional conflict can teach you the awesome art of returning non love with love. If you find yourself on the receiving end of an emotionally abusive pattern, your ability to love yourself and parent yourself can take a quantum leap. Such a leap can also lead to the spontaneous healing of the wound at the heart of the relationship. This does not in any way mean that such abuse is in any way appropriate. It is not.

In your relationships you will have to find the place of deepest guidance in your own heart. This will always tell you what to do. If an emotional pattern becomes unbearable, it is always a good idea to seek the guidance of a professional counsellor. Sometimes a third awareness can be a powerful leveller in a relationship, and it is certainly not a weakness to seek this out. On the contrary, it shows a great commitment to the love itself to seek help in loving more deeply.

There is a delicate balance to be struck when moving into your own Venus Sequence. This balance is about knowing where your own true boundaries lie. You can learn to love yourself more deeply through any situation, but you also have to know when to let go. The Venus Sequence will help you in finding this balance, and as you do so, you will feel the swelling of the great joy of your Purpose, bringing you a new core stability in life and a far greater level of surrender to the underground currents of your Dharma.

THE SHADOW

When contemplating your Purpose in relationships, the Shadow of this Gene Key and its lines will always tell you something very profound about your specific difficulties in relationships. It is so easy for us to lose a wider sense of

23

perspective when faced with the intensity of one-to-one relating. This Shadow will draw you again and again into the depths of the drama. It will force you into a role that you find very unsettling, and in addition to this it will probably make you feel guilty about the way you are behaving. Your inherent higher purpose is something that you can always sense deep within the cells, encoded in your DNA. So when this Shadow appears to lure you away from the better person you know you are and can be, it is very painful. When we get to know another person very intimately over time, there is no escaping that person seeing this Shadow side of your nature. This is why the beginning of relationships usually feel so good – because this Shadow has not yet presented itself.

When it finally does, then you really need to remember that this is your true work, and this is the deeper purpose of all true intimacy – to reflect back your inner Shadows in order that you can unlock their gifts and transform them.

THE GIFT

The Gift of your Purpose in relationships shifts your whole life onto another higher plane. When our relationships feel good, our whole life tends to move effortlessly. When your relationships are being harvested for the purpose of inner transformation, then it can seem as though anything in life is possible. We get a huge lift from the unlocking of the Gift of this Gene Key.

This Gift of higher purpose lies in the interactive field of every relationship on this planet. When two human auras combine, then an enormous amount of kinetic creative energy is released. This creativity actually comes through the interference pattern of the auric field. This is why it so often manifests as chaos and confusion, which tends to bring out the worst in us! However, inner transformation is the sifting and processing of all this colliding electromagnetic information. We have to process it at a quantum level, a chemical level, an emotional level and a mental level. That takes a great deal of awareness. As you enter into your Venus Sequence, you will begin to grasp the complexity of all these subtle levels of reality that overlap each other whenever we move towards true intimacy.

The Gift of the Gene Key relating to your Purpose emerges as your commitment to opening your heart deepens, no matter how intense the voltage of your relationships become. Gradually, you begin to retrain yourself out of your old reactive patterns, and rewire the inner pathways that dictate the way you relate to others. Your awareness cuts through your mental judgement, your emotional resentment, and your chemical overload. Your emotional challenges fuel your Core Stability. They knock you around until you take responsibility for your own drama, and surrender to your own Dharma. This is how you lay the foundation that allows for a permanent opening of your heart.

THE SIDDHI

The Siddhi of your Purpose in relationships can be summed up in a single word – Embodiment. In the Gene Keys, we talk of embodiment as a real life anchoring of the higher frequencies into the physical structure of our DNA. This is the highest purpose of all our relationships – to deliver the opportunity of a full awakening of our heart. You might like to consider the Gene Key of your Purpose in this light.

Because the Sphere of Purpose lies at the base of your Profile, everything else rests upon it. This means that your response to your daily dharma sets a resonant frequency that runs throughout the rest of your Profile. This is the meaning of the word 'Hologenetic'. It means that your awakening occurs in a subtle sequence as you open your heart to whatever comes your way. Only an authentic heart is capable of opening in this way. There is a direct relationship between your heart and the nucleotide sequences within DNA. We humans are pre-designed to awaken to these higher frequencies, and our dharma is the path that sets up this amazing possibility.

The ancient understanding of Tantra is an affirmation of this process of dual cultivation through our relationships that leads to higher states. This isn't so much about our sexuality, although it may involve a refining of our sexual and creative energies, but it is about the transmutation of patterns that do not support our heart in its opening. Each relationship has unique karmic patterns woven into the fabric of its chemistry, and the karma unravels as you deepen your level of embodiment. Eventually, as you move to transmute deeper and deeper Shadow patterns, a light begins to dawn inside you. This is the light of pure consciousness, and once you become aware of it, it can never be extinguished again.

THE 6 LINES OF YOUR PURPOSE IN RELATIONSHIPS

As we enter the Venus Sequence, you will see that each of the 6 lines has a low frequency keynote and a high frequency keynote. When we look at the Purpose in relationships, we also have the addition of a repressive tendency and a reactive tendency.

These are behavioural mirrors for you to consider as you look at your own relationship keynotes. Sometimes we react and sometimes we repress. It depends upon our culture, our conditioning, and the chemistry of the relationship itself which way we tend towards, and sometimes we shuffle between the two poles. The Venus Sequence is highly specific in this way, as it allows us to witness our Shadow patterns and their hidden potential Gifts in great depth.

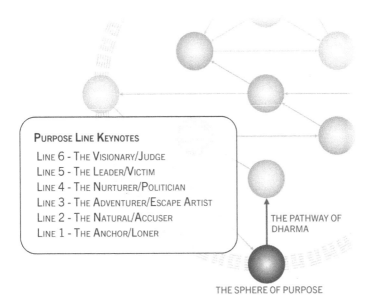

PURPOSE LINE KEYNOTES

LINE 6 - THE VISIONARY/JUDGE
LINE 5 - THE LEADER/VICTIM
LINE 4 - THE NURTURER/POLITICIAN
LINE 3 - THE ADVENTURER/ESCAPE ARTIST
LINE 2 - THE NATURAL/ACCUSER
LINE 1 - THE ANCHOR/LONER

THE PATHWAY OF DHARMA

THE SPHERE OF PURPOSE

Line 1: The Anchor / Loner

The Loner (Shadow)
Repressive Tendency: Not Standing up for yourself
Reactive Tendency: Forcing your point of view
Main Block: You are driven by your need to feel secure

The 1st line always carries this inward looking view, and when this emerges at the Shadow frequency, it becomes a habit of excluding those closest to us. The 1st line can be very self-absorbed in this way – so much so, that it often draws its emotional life so deeply inward, that it can no longer feel anything. This is the archetype of the loner. At the Shadow frequency, the loner is a pattern that may believe itself to be emotionally self-reliant. Other people's emotions can seem bothering and excessive to them. The truth is however that the 1st line that seems emotionally detached is usually driven by a profound need to feel secure, and at the first sign of conflict, they will unconsciously shut down.

A repressive expression of this Shadow might manifest as a quality of emotional 'hiding', or a fear of standing up for oneself rooted in a lack of Core Stability. On the other hand, the 1st line can also react very forcefully, pushing its view angrily at another in an attempt to make them stand down.

The Anchor (Gift)
Inner Strength: Standing up for yourself in a firm but kind way
Outer Strength: Listening to the needs of others
Highest Potential: Your confidence makes others feel secure

When you look at the 1st line through the lens of its Gift, you see a person transformed from the view we saw at the Shadow frequency. The purpose of your relationships is to become this person. The repressive tendency becomes your inner strength, which enables you to stand up for yourself while maintaining a kind and compassionate tone. The reactive tendency to bully another person becomes instead an innate ability to listen inwardly to one's own emotions, and therefore to be able to empathise with the emotional needs of others. The archetype of the Anchor is to stand in your Core Stability like an oak tree.

You will bend only so far as your boundaries allow, but you will also allow others to find their inner confidence in relationship to your strength and groundedness.

Line 2: The Natural / Accuser
The Accuser (Shadow)
Repressive Tendency: Burying your head in the sand
Reactive Tendency: Responding with angry outbursts
Main Block: You are unaware of your effect on others

You may recall that the 2nd line Purpose is about flow and posture, and is linked to the power of the spine. When this energy becomes blocked at the Shadow frequency, then the whole body loses its lustre and core strength.

Perhaps more than any other line, the 2nd line tends to get caught up in the charge of the emotional drama to such an extent, that they become almost blinded by emotion. The archetype of the Accuser refers to the 2nd line's habit of projecting their emotional pain onto someone else. At the root of their pain is their refusal to take responsibility for their own behaviour. This manifests either as a pattern of stubbornness that will not hear another's view (the repressive side), or a tendency towards aggressive and angry outbursts (the reactive side), that serves only to strengthen the distance between those involved. The great challenge for the 2nd line Shadow is to remember their natural sense of flow in emotional situations, and to allow others the space to share their feelings without being overwhelmed.

The Natural (Gift)
Inner Strength: Responding to life spontaneously
Outer Strength: Being at peace with others
Highest Potential: Your easy-going nature allows everyone around you to relax

It is often shocking and perhaps amusing for people to look at their potential emotional Gifts once they have seen the Shadows in action.

Often the higher frequency behaviour pattern is exactly the opposite from the Shadow! Here we see the archetype of the Natural. These are people whose nature is so in tune with the emotional realm that they make all relationships look easy. Instead of blocking their own potential the 2nd line rises up on the spontaneity of their heart.

No matter how powerful the emotions may feel, the 2nd line can find an easy and natural way of expressing them without in any way projecting them onto another. This deep emotional ease makes the 2nd line a natural magnet for people who feel emotionally insecure or stuck. The aura of a healthy 2nd line feels very comfortable to be around and their fluidity and sense of personal embodiment allows others to unwind, breathe, and settle into their spine.

Line 3: The Adventurer / Escape Artist

The Escape Artist (Shadow)
Repressive Tendency: Diverting attention away from yourself
Reactive Tendency: Creating emotional dramas
Main Block: You run away from making commitments in life

We have seen already that one of the main themes for the 3rd line is commitment: how to find continuity and commitment in a life that is wired to change? If you compare your life to those around you, you are likely to try and shape your life in a way that feels more secure and stable. And when this outer stability fails, as it likely will, you may end up feeling as though you are the failure. This can be a very painful process for the 3rd line.

Emotions are the lifeblood of relationships, and the 3rd line can feel overwhelmed by them at times, particularly if they have deep-seated feelings of unworthiness. This leads to the classic 3rd line archetype of the Escape Artist. In order to avoid feeling unworthy, the 3rd line develops all kinds of strategies for avoiding conflict. At the repressive level, this is really about diverting attention. This can be done in all kinds of ways, but one of the most common is through humour. The 3rd line has a natural gift of humour, but at the Shadow level this is often used as a diversion.

The 3rd line also has this gift of adaptability, which the Shadow will employ at an emotional level. This can make them very slippery and hard to pin down.

Even though the 3rd line Shadow will try their utmost to avoid anything that makes them feel uncomfortable, at the reactive level they end up creating all manner of situations that bring this about. Such a life can be very colourful to watch from the outside, but very painful when you are the one in the driving seat. When the 3rd line reacts emotionally, it tends to run away as fast as it can from the person or place where the pain took place. This can then become a habit of creating dramas, and then running away from them.

The Adventurer (Gift)
Inner Strength: Laughing at yourself
Outer Strength: Accepting the feelings of others
Highest Potential: Your enthusiasm for life is contagious

When the 3rd line Shadow themes are transformed by self awareness, we see a very different set of gifts emerging. Transformation is always rooted in self-honesty, which brings perspective, and with this comes an ability to laugh at yourself and the way that your dharma unravels. This is the 3rd line as an emotional adventurer. Relationships are such a rich part of the human experience, and once the 3rd line has overcome its fear of commitment, it learns a huge amount about life and people. The ability to laugh at oneself is a manifestation of compassion. Awareness always brings this inner sense of humour, because it shows you how human you are. You are fallible, and things do not always go the way you expect them to. As long as you stay committed to your own honesty and to being authentic, then life can be such a great adventure.

This ability to enjoy the uncertainty of life brings a deep sense of inner trust alive in you. It is where your enthusiasm springs from. This is why others will begin to trust in you, without always wanting more from you. It is always down to you just 'staying in the room', instead of trying to find a way to escape.

Line 4: The Politician / Nurturer

The Politician (Shadow)
Repressive Tendency: Being emotionally numb
Reactive Tendency: Cutting others off in a cruel way
Main Block: You reject others before they can reject you

The Shadow of the 4th line is the Politician. The 4th line has the ability to use its considerable social gifts to conceal its own inner fear and/or hurt. The 3rd and 4th lines are the most obviously emotional of all the 6 lines. However, at the Shadow frequency they both represent patterns that might seem the least emotional, because they both use different means to try and avoid conflict and pain.

The 3rd line may run, but the 4th line pretends that they are fine. During challenging emotional exchanges, they may experience their heart closing off and their whole being turning emotionally numb. This numbness allows their mind to take control and manage the situation at the expense of the emotions. It is important to remember that none of these Shadow patterns are anyone's fault. They are not deliberate. They are the unconscious genetic coping mechanisms we learned as children. So when the 4th line heart becomes numb, it isn't because they want it to. No one wants to have a closed heart. However, this does mean that the 4th line can appear very cold when they speak from this numb place inside.

The Nurturer (Gift)
Inner Strength: Being gentle with yourself
Outer Strength: Connecting deeply with others
Highest Potential: Your generous spirit enables others to accept themselves

Out of every one of these Shadow patterns comes a Gift. In the case of the 4th line, it is the ability to parent yourself with gentleness and patience. Because the 4th line has a tendency to feel emotionally numb when put in a vulnerable position, they can also learn how to bring themselves out of this state.

They do this through first of all accepting that they have shut off through no deliberate fault of their own. They then can either ask for gentle support, or if the other is unable to give that, they can withdraw and give it to themselves.

Out of this awareness of how to re-open your own heart come the many great Gifts of the 4th line – the ability to teach others how to do the same for example, or the ability to be openly vulnerable and to communicate authentically when experiencing emotional pain. All of these gifts lend the 4th line a quality of softness combined with great inner strength, which makes them the great nurturers of others.

Line 5: The Victim / Leader

The Victim (Shadow)
Repressive Tendency: Being lost in self pity
Reactive Tendency: Making others feel like the victim
Main Block: You create a web of illusions that keeps you trapped in your mind

The 5th line represents the Victim. In effect, all Shadow states of consciousness are indicative of a victim mentality, but the 5th line captures the essence of this role. We may recall that the 5th line Purpose has to do with the voice, which is why this is also the archetype of the leader. The repressive tendency of this line often manifests as a complaining tone. The 5th line gets stuck feeling sorry for itself, and can unconsciously create a whole reality around why they are worthy of your pity. This is a negative means of trying to get attention and love. On the other hand the reactive tendency, fuelled by anger, uses the voice to belittle others and make them feel small. This pattern will see others as the victim, and take advantage of their weaker position or less confident character. Both of these patterns come from an inner attitude that is usually built up over time.

The Leader (Gift)
Inner Strength: Seeing things clearly for yourself
Outer Strength: Using your clarity to help others
Highest Potential: Your practical mind makes you a strong and natural leader

The 5th line has to break through some deep-seated inner barriers in order to unlock its highest potential in life. At the Shadow frequency, it can be trapped by its own unconscious attitude based on individual survival. When this attitude is dismantled through deep self-awareness, the 5th line emerges triumphantly with all the qualities necessary to be a true leader. The first of these is the inner strength to see clearly into one's own being. This is the very insight that lifts the 5th line out of the victim mentality.

It also allows the 5th line to help others pull themselves out of the same difficulty. The Shadow frequency lies across our planet like a great blanket. When the 5th line awakens, the first thing it wants to do is free others from being co-dependent victims, and help them to be authentic emotionally independent adults. The magnetic power of the voice of an awakened 5th line can draw many people in for help, and the practical mind of the 5th line can furthermore deliver potent solutions. This is the 5th line operating at its best.

Line 6: The Judge / Visionary

The Judge (Shadow)
Repressive Tendency: Being uninterested and aloof
Reactive Tendency: Disempowering others through the intellect
Main Block: You exclude yourself through your judgement of everything and everyone

The 6th line carries a sense of detachment that sets it apart from all the other lines. This can be its strength and its downfall. At the Shadow frequency the 6th line never manages to come down from its objective perspective, but remains aloof and distant. This is a classic 6th line coping mechanism ensuring that all emotional exchanges are funnelled through the mind.

This can give 6th line people an air of aloofness or arrogance, and can make others think they are out of touch with their feelings. The reactive tendency here is all about using one's intellect to disempower others, although this is often not done deliberately. The 6th line Shadow can feel completely unemotional at times, and has an ability to analyse other people's emotions without being emotionally engaged themselves. This can lead to a sense of deep isolation in the 6th line.

The Visionary (Gift)
Inner Strength: Including yourself at every level of life
Outer Strength: Being a role model for others
Highest Potential: Your trust in life helps others to trust themselves

One of the key words for the 6th line Gift is Trust. They have to learn to trust in other people and to trust in their own process, which can include trusting in their own lack of feeling. As one's awareness comes more deeply into the body, the 6th line begins to realise that the mind rarely has the answer they think it does. The 6th line Gift emerges with patience. As a 6th line you have to measure things over time. It takes time for your emotions to surface, so you have to let other people know that you often don't know how you feel yet. When you do give yourself time, then you find a whole new part of your being coming alive. Your feelings provide such a depth of insight that you let go of your habit of going straight into your mind, and you learn to include yourself in relational processes instead of watching them from the outside. At this advanced stage, your mind works in harmony with your feelings, and this is where your Gift of Vision comes from – it emerges out of the intent of your cells, from deep inside your body. The 6th line has an amazing sensitivity to the unfolding rhythms of life, so it always brings with it a sense of deep trust in the timing of events. This attunement to the deep wisdom of the body, in turn makes the 6th line a natural person to go to for advice about anything in life.

CONTEMPLATING YOUR PURPOSE IN RELATIONSHIPS

You may now begin to have an inkling of the difference between working with your Activation Sequence and diving into your Venus Sequence. Your Venus Sequence provides you with an enormous depth of insight to contemplate. It's important again to be patient with this knowledge. Sometimes you may read a line that does not seem to belong to you, but it resonates very deeply nonetheless. As you go on deeper into the Venus Stream, you may find that line occurring at a deeper level. Understanding your Venus Sequence is rather like cracking the code of a safe.

There are various combinations and sequences that you have to move through before the door swings open. It is also worth mentioning that each of the lines offers up its wisdom to you regardless of your Profile. The further you go into this knowledge the less you will tend to worry about your external Profile. Sometimes wisdom is mysterious, and finds its way to you in an indirect and surprising fashion. Once again I would remind you of the importance of slowing down inside yourself in order for your contemplation to digest, sift, and filter your personal truth from this material.

The uniqueness of the Golden Path is that it is such an interior voyage of transformation. There is a paradox here, because although we are now travelling through the emotional landscape of our relationships, we are also treading a very private path. Only your awareness can do this work. Your relationships simply provide you with a useful mirror.

Even though you may wish to share your insights with your partner or those closest to you, the Venus Stream urges you inwards rather than outwards. It keeps calling you back to be a witness of your own internal world. It is very easy for us to be drawn back into the drama of our emotional lives.

The truth is that most communication in relationships takes place without words. We exchange chemical signals through the invisible electromagnetic currents and impulses of the aura. Our thoughts, intent, and feelings are always conveyed through time and space before we are usually even consciously aware of them.

In most relationships we put a lot of time and effort into trying to communicate our inner state of unfulfilment. But that unfulfilment is our own deep issue, and it is difficult to find one's way out of such a state through heated conversation.

The intensity of emotions can be a beautiful phenomenon. Even uncomfortable feelings can be appreciated at a certain level. This is certainly one of the goals of the Venus Sequence – to break us out of the habit of being completely hooked by the surface dramas of our lives.

If we learn not to take the bait in the first place, then we find there is a deeper calm to be found within. Out of this calm, a more candid and lucid form of communication is possible.

A dialogue out of one's depths is a rare and precious thing. It takes a person with great self love and inner patience to access this deeper sphere beneath the daily drama.

4. THE SPHERE OF ATTRACTION

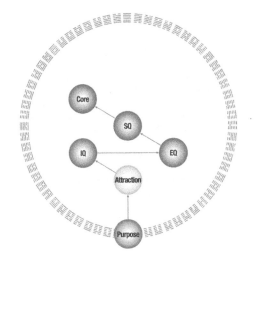

THE SPHERE OF ATTRACTION

In the Sphere of Attraction, we come into a place where chemistry governs all. In your Hologenetic Profile, this Gene Key is calculated by a specific position of the moon while you are still in your mother's womb. It is in many ways a portal to another world – the so-called 'astral plane'. The astral plane is an esoteric term that refers to the world where emotional currents have a living reality of their own. Here desires are born. This is the font of our sexuality, which is why it is about attraction. It is about the electromagnetic resonance of our dharma drawing in the etheric ingredients that will eventually manifest our destiny. The Sphere of Attraction sits like a fulcrum between the Pathways of Dharma and Karma. That which is encoded in our DNA as purpose rings out into the subtle planes, and calls in those relationships that offer us the greatest possibility of fulfilling our higher purpose. How we listen and learn from those relationships is up to us.

Relationship chemistry is one of the greatest unknown mysteries of our age. We are ruled by the chemistry of our relationships while at the same time having little understanding of their underlying forces. The chemistry between any two human beings creates a dynamic interactive energy field. When we are able to listen inwardly to what our relationships are telling us in silence, we may discover an incredible universe that we never realised existed. There are miracles waiting in the spaces between us, if we only knew how to harvest them.

When you enter the Venus Stream, you are invited into a very deep contemplation of your primary relationships. By this we mean your children, parents, spouses, lovers - anyone who lives and shares their life with you. You are invited to explore these relationships at a deeper level than you have ever considered possible. This is not necessarily about a change in your external dialogue (although that may also change), but it is about a change in your internal dialogue – the way your body, mind, and emotions respond internally to others. The Venus Stream asks you to listen carefully to your chemical responses without any judgement.

We are not looking for answers when we do this. This is not about analysis. We are simply receiving the other person's aura at the level at which it is meant to be taken in. We can even begin this work when the other person is absent, although their physical presence is necessary to fully learn from the relationship.

You should pay particular attention to those relationships which you find challenging or uncomfortable. The aura of such relationships usually contains a deeper vein of chemical information that is often rarely accessed due to the eruption of drama on the surface. When your awareness is able to dig deeper into such relationships, you often find that they contain the greatest diamonds, since they offer you the opportunity for inner transformation. It's often in the deep Shadows that the miracles lie hidden.

THE ATTRACTOR FIELD

In recent years, there has been much talk in esoteric circles about harnessing the attractor field that surrounds humans. Much of this information is geared towards the manifestation of one's wishes on the material plane. The Venus Sequence does not offer any such techniques for manifestation. It is unlikely that we humans really know what is good for us in the first place! What you do learn from this wisdom is that in life you will always get exactly what you need when you need it. The secret is not about asking for something in the future – it is about mining the full depth and splendour of what you already have in the present.

What is it that you wish for? More money? A perfect relationship? The ideal home? It's important to look at your present circumstances, and see how much there is to be grateful for. What is this something in the future that you seek? Such longings (whatever form they take) are very human and very understandable. You do not have to stop yourself from wishing for a happier life. But perhaps through yielding to the Venus Stream, you will see that happiness isn't really the grail that you are seeking. Your Attractor Field emerges out of the needs of your Dharma, your destiny.

Although it may be possible to tinker with your Attractor Field, the things you think you want will most probably not lead to fulfilment.

THE ATTRACTOR FIELD

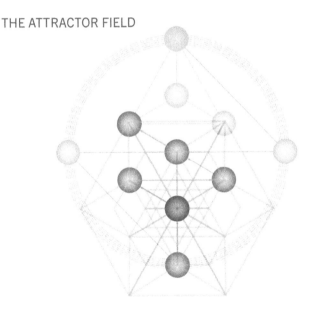

Our Attractor Field ripples out into the cosmos. It emerges through our deep desires. As you learn to see inwardly into your own astral body, you will discover layer upon layer of desires. When we get down to the bottom, we all find the same thing – the longing to express our true nature as unconditional love. Few are the humans who commit themselves fully to this path. Desires can be so wonderfully distracting! The Venus Stream invites you to explore the layers of wounding that cause us to break off from following this path by allowing ourselves to be distracted by the outer drama of our lives.

THE SEXUAL WOUND

In many of the ancient creation myths from around the world, we see a common theme involving a process of sexual wounding. One of the deepest human joys and challenges is the nature of our sexuality. We each carry a sexual theme into the world that dictates the kind of relationships we draw towards ourselves. It is also important to note that one's birth time needs to be fairly accurate, in order to see precisely which of the variations of Attractor Field you have in your Profile. If therefore you resonate more strongly to one or other of the lines, then you should trust your intuition above and beyond the Profile itself. It is always of great merit to read and contemplate each of the 6 lines, as they all contain universal truths applicable to us all.

Your sexual line theme is not only about the sexual act, but can be seen as a general theme relating to your vital energy, health, and your relationship to the creative process. This is why you may wish to contemplate the following keynotes in as wide a sense as possible. Obviously you can also contemplate how these themes may have played out in your past, and how certain relationships came into your life at certain times to teach you certain lessons. The important thing is to look as deeply as possible into the currents that drive your desire nature. When you learn to love yourself and the nature of the wound you carry, then you can witness the healing of that wound as a personal transformation.

GENTLENESS — THE SECRET OF SEXUAL HEALING

When moving into contemplation of your sexuality at such a deep level, the most important quality to remember at all times is gentleness. Many issues coupled with our sexuality occurred when we were young and lacking in experience and wisdom. As we move further along the Golden Path, we will be journeying into the cycles of our childhood in depth, but for now the essential ingredient to add to the mix is tenderness. There are knots woven into our DNA that will only yield to the very softest touch. You will therefore have to be the tenderest parent to yourself as you step into this terrain.

No one else has the capacity to heal these places inside at the level that you do. Indeed, just remembering this self-gentleness over and over again may well be enough to bring healing to your heart and body.

THE SHADOW

When contemplating the Shadow of the Gene Key relating to your Attractor Field, it is an opportunity for you to look into the subtle layers of your desire. You can consider this at a sexual level and a material level. How has this Shadow played out in your life? How is it playing out today? Consider the disturbance that this Shadow may have caused you and others. There is no need for blame or guilt here. We all carry a fractal aspect of the great sacred wound. Our path through life is about coming to terms with this imperfect part of our nature. Our sexuality makes us feel so vulnerable, but equally we can also hide behind it. Everything in the world is rooted in sex, because everything penetrates everything else at a quantum level.

At one level, sex takes place whenever two auras interact, regardless of sexuality or age. This is the merging of the creative electromagnetic field of every relationship. Look deeply therefore into this Shadow, and be willing to feel the vulnerability of your theme, and how it is trying to find wholeness in the outer world.

THE GIFT

The Gift emerges as your awareness cuts through the projections of your sexuality, and finds the place of innocent vulnerability that is inside every one of us. In vulnerability lies great strength. This does not mean that you have to go around expressing your vulnerability – rather that you own it as a private interior wisdom that belongs to you alone. If you decide to express it, then it needs the right environment and person to receive it. Your vulnerability connects you more closely to everyone else's vulnerability, no matter how hardened they are on the surface, and this makes you a naturally more compassionate person.

It is an amazing revelation to begin seeing the people in the world around you as innocent children all with this same wound at the heart of their being. This kind of shift in your attitude relays a very different chemical signal through your Attractor Field, and you will undoubtedly find that the whole outer landscape of your life will also change to reflect this transformation.

THE SIDDHI

The Siddhi of your sexuality involves a profound spiritual transformation. Beneath the Gene Keys revelation lies a body of teachings known as the Corpus Christi. This encapsulates the higher teachings of spiritual Initiation, and describes the nature of the subtle bodies. Within this Corpus of teachings and transmissions, we learn about the specific process that occurs as a person's frequency becomes more and more refined. At a certain stage known as the 5th Initiation, the sexual energy at the core of our being is transformed in a tantric phenomenon known mystically as the Annunciation. This is directly linked to the transformation of our lower astral nature into its higher counterpart known as the buddhic body. The Siddhi of your Sexuality governs this extraordinary alchemical process. It is at this stage that your Attractor Field begins to operate at its highest level, drawing in the most refined and exquisite frequencies from your greater self. This leads to a phase of prolonged transmutation, which is often also accompanied by states of ecstasy.

THE 6 LINES OF YOUR SEXUALITY (THE SPHERE OF ATTRACTION)

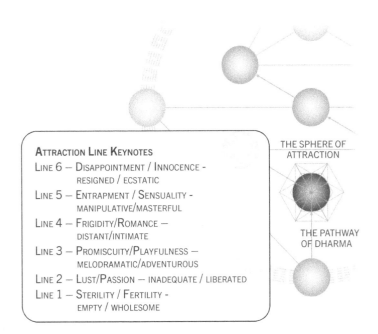

ATTRACTION LINE KEYNOTES

LINE 6 — DISAPPOINTMENT / INNOCENCE - RESIGNED / ECSTATIC

LINE 5 — ENTRAPMENT / SENSUALITY - MANIPULATIVE/MASTERFUL

LINE 4 — FRIGIDITY/ROMANCE — DISTANT/INTIMATE

LINE 3 — PROMISCUITY/PLAYFULNESS — MELODRAMATIC/ADVENTUROUS

LINE 2 — LUST/PASSION — INADEQUATE / LIBERATED

LINE 1 — STERILITY / FERTILITY - EMPTY / WHOLESOME

THE SPHERE OF ATTRACTION

THE PATHWAY OF DHARMA

44444

Line 1: Sterility / Fertility - Empty / Wholesome

Each of the following lines has a general theme and an accompanying state. Depending on the frequency of your inner attitude, you can see how both play out in your life at a low frequency and a high frequency. The 1st line of the hexagram always conveys the essence of the whole topic, and here we can see it is about Sterility or Fertility. Our Dharma offers us so many opportunities to be creative with our lives. There is always a fertile response to every situation. On the other hand, the Shadow consciousness is depletive rather than abundant. Sterility can be applied to any human sphere – you can be spiritually sterile, financially sterile, socially sterile, emotionally sterile, and of course sexually sterile.

Sterility leads naturally to disease, because it involves the blocking of the natural life force through the body.

This leads to experiences that are perceived as devoid of meaning, and which therefore drain us and leave us feeling empty rather than full. States of depression or exhaustion follow naturally out of the Shadow of this first line. Our modern world offers a cornucopia of distractions for our desires, from excessive materialism to overstimulation of our body and senses. Many of these leave us feeling empty and sterile, closing down our attractor field and locking us into tight, unimaginative little lives. Relationships lived through the low frequency of this line will soon seem sterile and dull, lacking the lustre of hope and joy that they might once have had.

The higher frequency of this 1st line is anything but sterile. It is a rippling field of pure unbridled potential. If you have a 1st line sexuality, then you are a hub of creative forces. You will attract relationships that are dynamic – they may not always be easy – but they will have a potent and fertile aura, out of which much beauty can arise. The difference between a sterile and a fertile relationship is always your attitude. Every

48

relationship has the potential to be a wonderful adventure. If the lustre has faded, then it is down to your own perception.

You will have to open your heart up again to life, rather than blaming the relationship. This re-awakening can occur in any relationship. Fertility is about seeing life at a higher frequency. It is about seeing the whole of a person, rather than only the Shadow or even only the Gift. This is when a relationship becomes wholesome – when it includes the Shadow, and the Shadow is embraced and transformed. Only then can the higher purpose of the relationship be realised, and only then can the attractor field draw in the elements that support you in living your life at a higher frequency.

Line 2: Lust / Passion – Inadequate / Liberated

The roots of human desire run deep. There are many forms and frequencies of desire. Our most basic desire is the desire that drives us to mate. This is a genetic pressure inside us that rises and falls according to our distinct hormonal cycles. However, this evolutionary impulse to procreate also gets entangled with other forms of desire – for example, the desire to escape our suffering. Our unconscious desire to escape suffering is the foundation of the Shadow frequency, and it drives us into endless cycles of pain and pleasure. Many of our relationships come as a result of us following our sexual desires, which is perfectly natural. However, when this becomes mixed in with our desire to escape suffering, perhaps in the form of an unrealistic romantic projection, our relationships can very quickly become difficult and disappointing.

The 2nd line of the hexagram is in many ways the most expressive of its essence. At the Shadow frequency, this means that the 2nd line will always express as lust, which is the blending of sexual desire and fear. Lust on its own has a kind of animal purity, but when coupled with deep unconscious fear it becomes unstable, and a person in its thrall becomes blind to their own feelings and the feelings of others. This is sex used as a weapon against fear, or as a distraction from fear and deep discomfort. The deepest fear that drives the Shadow states is the fear of our own death – the fear of non-existence. For example when the Hindus describe the endless cycles of rebirth that we humans move through, they are describing our desperation to escape this primal fear. The fear exists inside us at a cellular level, so we can never escape it through any external strategy.

The 2nd line must therefore come to know the deeper force that drives its sexuality – the hunger to escape one's own discomfort. At its source, this is felt as a potent sense of inadequacy. Even though such people can be very comfortable within their sexuality, their real fear is of the depth of their own feelings, or the fear of feeling nothing at all. Such fears are responsible for their feelings of inadequacy.

If you therefore have a 2nd line sexuality, you must get in touch with this sense of inadequacy, otherwise it will always prevent you from experiencing a truly fulfilling relationship. It is easy for the 2nd line to hide behind their sexuality, and continue a life where sex becomes nothing more than a temporary release of the pressure of this deep fear.

As you contemplate your Gene Key and its line theme within this Sphere of Attraction, you may have to move into uncharted waters as you touch hidden places within your psyche, both within yourself and possibly with your partner. You will have to get in touch with your vulnerability, and this requires patience and a very soft touch. You will have to remember to tread slowly and go gently into this highly sensitive territory. When you do touch your own sense of inadequacy, know that you have hit upon the real treasure. There is no pressure to do anything other than wrap it in awareness. You may also have to break one of your deepest habits – the use of your sexuality as a means of escaping from your true feelings. However, when the ice begins to melt, then the same energy will reemerge, but instead of being filtered through fear, it will carry the vibration of love, and this will be expressed in your life as passion.

The 2nd line sexuality can experience a powerful liberation through their desire nature as their true passion emerges for the first time in an open-hearted way. An open-hearted 2nd line leads to a life lived with great passion, and the passion will tend to move to higher and higher levels of frequency. Once fear is seen and accepted, our desire transforms from the urge to escape suffering into the yearning to feel and express deeper love. A truly healthy 2nd line sexuality will burn with an intense wish to know one's own higher nature, which will at the same time be balanced by a pervasive gentle compassion for the nature of the human sexual wound.

Line 3: Promiscuity / Playfulness – Elodramatic / Adventurous

The 3rd line sexuality can have 2 possible expressions at the Shadow frequency. While one is expressive and promiscuous, the other may be repressive and locked. The 3rd line is naturally warm and playful, but sometimes because of certain relationships that are drawn into one's attractor field, the 3rd line may have a painful early sexual experience that has the effect of freezing one's sexuality. The healing of such a deep-seated wound may be beyond the scope of the Golden Path Program, as it may involve help from an open-hearted therapist specialising in these kinds of trauma. In such cases, the first step in healing is to accept that one needs help, and to begin the journey of finding that help. Like each of the 6 lines, the 3rd line has its own particular path of healing. As was stated earlier, the combination of self-awareness and inner tenderness towards oneself can bring hidden wounds to the surface, where they can be healed and transformed.

The expressive Shadow of the 3rd line will tend towards promiscuity, which always leads to melodrama. The 3rd line often creates a complex life for itself with many broken relationships and disappointments. Unlike the 2nd line of lust, the 3rd line is in some ways more addicted to the drama of the chase than the actual sexual act itself. The 3rd line Shadow likes to titillate and run. It will display open-heartedness right up until the point of commitment, and then it will close off and run away. We need to remember that these patterns are unconscious inside us. They are the many ways in which we do our best to handle our desire nature. There can be no blame, because we inherit such patterns from our culture and conditioning. The 3rd line desperately wants to be in a committed open-hearted relationship, but at the same time it keeps undermining itself. The trick is to become aware of the unconscious patterns that drive us. The moment we can see the pattern, we cease to be a victim of it.

The 3rd line sexuality needs to temper their life with a good sense of humour. This is not a disparaging kind of humour, but a tender-hearted ability to laugh at one's own dramas. When we can begin to look at our own lives as we might read a good Jane Austen novel, we begin to realise that we no longer need be the unwitting pawns of the dramas played out by our genes. Of all the lines, the 3rd line needs this perspective the most. Once you can see that you have been trying to escape your own heart, you can see how futile and ridiculous a thing this is! At this point, you will become more playful. A healthy 3rd line sexuality will indeed be experimental and adventurous, but not at the expense of your heart or the hearts of others. With awareness, you will be able to see your heart opening and closing all on its own, but you won't have to think that there is anything wrong with you. This means that you can stay in a relationship, and still have the adventure of healing. You will only ever be able to heal your heart in a committed relationship that is accepting of vulnerability.

No matter which line you have activated in your Profile, you will need this ability to forgive yourself when your heart temporarily closes off. We each need to learn the gentle art of self-parenting. This involves the ability to caress your own heart back into life. Often this must be done alone, as we let go of the pain and blame, and allow ourselves to feel safe once again. Whenever we blame another for our own hurt, we are making ourselves into a victim. Although our hurt may well be triggered by another person's insensitivity, our first goal is to be able to nurture our heart back into openness. Once we have mastered this art, which is the art made possible at the Gift frequency, we can move on to the final goal of keeping our heart open all the time, no matter what, which is the realm of the Siddhis.

Line 4: Frigidity / Romance – Distant / Intimate

The 4th line really encapsulates the theme of self-parenting. In this sense, we can all learn a deep lesson from the 4th line process. The low frequency keynote of the 4th line is 'frigidity', and its state is about being emotionally distant. So many relationships move in this direction. The juice and excitement dries up at a certain stage, and the two people drift apart. Frigidity can take place on many levels. The relationship can become monotonous and get bogged down in the many demands of everyday life and responsibility. The raising of children for example can put a great demand on any relationship, often driving a wedge between a couple who once felt deeply in love.

There is nothing that creates more distance in a relationship than the untransformed Shadow patterns of each partner. If there is no sense of higher purpose to the relationship, then the Shadow patterns may well strangle the love at the heart. If there is no way of understanding the Shadow and transforming its energy, then the icy world of resentment and conflict will inevitably set in. Nowhere is this more clearly seen, than in the 4th line expression. The healthy 4th line is all warmth and friendliness, but in its Shadow manifestation it becomes distant and cold. The human heart feeds on intimacy, and true intimacy involves vulnerability. The 4th line Shadow has a knack of switching off the warmth in a relationship often without even realising it.

The 4th line Shadow often manifests through tone. Couples experiencing deep conflict are usually exceptionally sensitive to the tone of each other's voice. A cold tone can have an instant triggering effect on another person's openness. The 4th line Shadow therefore needs to become aware of the kind of tone they use by gauging the feedback from their partner. In the Introduction to the Venus Sequence, we learned how every relationship acts as a mirror, and this is always true. Your relationship to your partner shows you your relationship to your own heart. How you handle this mirror is the great topic of the Venus Sequence. When you are able to accept personal responsibility for your own expression, whether conscious or unconscious, you have begun the great journey of transformation.

When the 4th line realises how frosty and distant it is being, and is able to let go of blaming the other for their state, then they have taken the first and most important step in self-parenting. Now they know that only they have the power to bring love back into their heart. The 4th line keynote is Romance, because it needs to find gentle, creative ways to romance itself. Of course the 4th line in pain will also respond well to another person coming to them gently and with warmth and understanding. As is so often the case with all manner of inner difficulties, the 4th line also needs to be approached with great patience and calm, in the spirit of open-heartedness. When they emerge from their hurt, they will exude gratefulness and warmth, as though their whole aura were an invitation to intimacy.

The healthy 4th line sexuality will also very likely wish to express its love through words as well as through their physicality. As we have seen earlier in the Activation Sequence, this 4th line is all about the breath and communication. It is through the 4th line that the great words of love always come into the world.

Line 5: Entrapment / Sensuality –
Anipulative / Masterful

Like all the lines, the 5th line may express itself in either a repressive/passive manner and/or in a reactive/aggressive manner. The grand theme of the 5th line sexuality is Entrapment, and this can be seen on many levels. The more repressed version of this theme is about being a victim of your own low self-esteem. The 5th line Shadow continually worries about what others think about it. Sexually this can lead to many unhealthy patterns – perhaps you become obsessed with pleasing others at the expense of your own feelings or needs. On the other hand, perhaps you allow your fears to entrap you in a belief that you can never satisfy your partner, which then becomes a self-fulfilling prophecy.

When you consider your individual line theme alongside its Gene Key, then the story will eventually become clear to you. All 5th line Shadow themes are about being ensnared in a false mental projection field unconsciously created by your own fears.

The reactive version of the 5th line Shadow expresses itself through a more extrovert nature. It can use sex unconsciously to manipulate others, again through the creation of a false mental projection field. These are people who may seem more than comfortable with their sexuality, and who can use it to entrap others in an unconscious game of power or politics. Beneath this pattern is a deep fear of true intimacy, and often a tender wound that may have occurred in one's youth. The 5th line weaves a web of self-delusion that can project great self-confidence, but that feels very insecure. Once a 5th line person begins to admit to their true vulnerability, feeling it inside the body, their whole belief system about who they are can be shattered. This is often a delicate process that requires patience and sensitive support.

For the 5th line, the process of waking up can be fairly dramatic as one's entire worldview is built up over years around the grain of these false beliefs and projections. When we first see how delicate our inner world really is, it can be alarming. It can also be very empowering to let go of who we think we are, and step fully into a present moment undefined by our past experience. The 5th line has an inherent gift for sensuality, which is why so much of its worldview is based around its relationship to sexuality. If you have a 5th line sexuality, above all you will have to learn about having crystal clear boundaries. You will exude a powerful sensuality no matter what you do, so it is vital that you learn to accept, enjoy, and appreciate the beauty of this, rather than becoming a victim of it, either through an over-contraction or an over-expansion.

The healthy 5th line is masterful in how they deal with their sexuality in the world. It becomes a part of their charm and grace without being in any way unnatural. Within their intimate relationships, the 5th line can experience the full power and beauty of their sexuality, and it can become a powerful healing and self-empowering force. In their outer life, sexuality becomes sensuality – it carries a natural appropriateness wherever it goes – it is vivacious without being misleading, playful without being seductive, and mysterious without being bewitching. It is the perfect expression of a healthy sexuality at play in the world.

Line 6: Disappointment / Innocence –
Resigned / Ecstatic

The 6th line can often feel like it carries the weight of all the other lines within its process. In the Activation Sequence we saw that it is the line of Vision, and to arrive at that Vision, it must move through a lifetime of experiences that are varied enough to support such a far-reaching view. At the Shadow frequency, the 6th line can therefore be very confusing. The vision beats deep within our DNA, but it doesn't seem to manifest externally. It often emerges only to collapse back again, leaving the 6th line disappointed at such a deep level that they can give up on life altogether. When you apply this process to our sexuality, one can quite easily imagine the kind of things that might occur.

The 6th line often has a foretaste of their highest potential when they are young. In relationships they may fall deeply in love with someone, only to see this fade or crash or burn up, leaving an emptiness behind. Of course all romantic love is like this, and most human beings experience this at some level in their lives. Each of the 6 lines carries a universal theme that is applicable to us all. The difference with the 6th line is that at some level they cannot give up on the dream. Nothing the 6th line does can kill the dream inside. For this reason, the 6th line sexuality may have completely resigned itself to the belief that their dreams are unrealistic. Mentally and even emotionally, they may have given up hope of ever connecting with another person at the level they once dreamed of, even though at a purely physical level, their DNA still carries the promise of more.

What all of this means is that every time the 6th line engages at a sexual level, somewhere inside they feel a kind of cosmic disappointment. The lessons they must therefore learn are patience and perspective. We have to accept and trust the stage we have reached in our process. The 6th line moreover has to straddle two worlds – they must accept what they have in the moment, but they will also wish for more. It is this wish for more that needs to be translated into a subtle impulse in their lives. It is not designed to be repressed. The impulse to grow, evolve, and learn lies at the heart of every healthy relationship.

For the 6th line, this impulse must be trained inwardly into one's own process of heart expansion. One must tread carefully here, because the wish for more can be so easily aimed at one's partner where it is readily turned into blame. We blame the other for not being open enough to love at the level we wish. In fact, it is usually us that are not open enough. If we were open enough, then we would also allow our partner to love at the level that they are currently capable of. Therefore the safest and most natural place for the wish for more is to use it as a means to become the very model of open-heartedness that you have always dreamed of.

It is intriguing that so many people dream of experiencing greater love in their relationships, but for the most part they project this wish onto their partner as a wish that they might change. The secret of this 6th line is the secret of the whole Venus Sequence process:

We can use non-love to create more love.

This is the heart of the Venus Sequence - this gift of turning the challenges in our relationships into an inner teaching that widens our capacity to love. The moment you can use your discomfort for the purpose of inner transformation, is the moment you transcend your disappointment. The final goal of the 6th line, and therefore all relationships, is to rediscover the heart of our own innocence. This means we must embrace every fear, every anger, every trace of guilt, blame, or any negative charge, and use it as a fierce inner lens to focus the power of our own self love. You may see that the natural state of the healthy 6th line is to be ecstatic.

To be ecstatic means to be as a child, to be surrounded by the halo of our own innocence, and to cavort in the field of unconditional love that is our true nature. And to be ecstatic means more than this – it also means that we are living the vision inside our hearts, instead of projecting it onto the world around us. We no longer blame those around us for our feelings of non-love, but use every grain of Shadow as a means of sculpting more ecstasy from the living clay of our relationships.

CONTEMPLATING THE SPHERE OF ATTRACTION IN YOUR RELATIONSHIPS

When you have read each of the 6 lines of Sexuality, you will have a good general view of how these lines work within all relationships. As has been said already in this book, if you find that a certain line has a strong resonance for you, but does not appear in your Profile, you should trust your intuition above and beyond the Profile. Life is filled with mysteries, and sometimes we do not see the whole picture until later on in our contemplation.

The entire art of Contemplation is to put aside any predefined ideas or notions you may have around a certain subject. Sexuality is one of the most charged subjects of all, so it's a good idea to surround it with a sense of spaciousness, both mentally and emotionally, as you dive into its mysteries.

As you contemplate the Sphere of your Attraction, you might like to think about the power of your attractor field, and how it keeps bringing certain relationships into your life. See if you can find the common thread that runs through each and every one of these relationships. What is your greatest lesson? What is your dharma trying to show you, and at what level are you listening to it? Your sexuality exists in a pure form outside of your past and your future. Its nature is innocence. How can you regain that innocence? Much of our challenges with sexuality are rooted in our past, and in the worldview we have evolved because of that past.

The great challenge is to look upon yourself with fresh eyes, and to move deeper into your own vulnerability without demanding anyone else has to go there with you. Since you are no longer a child, you now have the opportunity to be a gentle and nurturing parent for yourself. Like any child, you need a combination of tenderness with firm boundaries.

Above all, it may help you to enter into contemplation of your sexuality if you enter in playfully, without instantly tensing up. If you do tense up and feel constriction, then take a pause, breathe into the difficulty, withdraw safely if necessary, and then bring your heart back to life in your own time, without blame and with compassion. The more frequently you do this, the easier it will become. Be gentle with yourself, and find your own rhythm, as you go about this powerful life-changing work.

5. THE PATHWAY OF KARMA

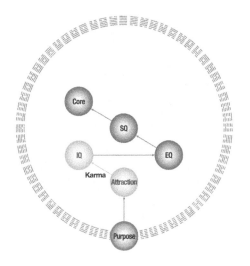

THE PATHWAY OF KARMA

Flowing out of the Sphere of Attraction and linking into the Sphere of IQ, we find the Pathway of Karma. There is naturally an important relationship between these two themes of dharma and karma. Putting it simply, your dharma manifests in your life through your karma, and your karma is released by means of your Attractor Field. In order to fully understand these relationships, we need first of all to know what we mean by the word 'karma'.

As we have seen, your dharma can be seen as your relationship to your life path. It indicates the level of your surrender to the great forces that shape all lives. As you evolve and refine your frequency, so your karma adjusts itself to the needs of your higher purpose.

When you begin to transform the Shadow frequencies within your DNA, then you attract in new kinds of relationships, or you attract new higher elements into your existing relationships. Every relationship contains a repository of karma for you to transform. If you decide to turn away from the relationship, you will only meet the karma again in the next relationship, albeit in a different form. As we move into the Venus Sequence, we find ourselves dancing in a world of subtle frequencies. The Pathway of Dharma sets the tone, the Sphere of Attraction calls in the relationship, and the Pathway of Karma offers you the opportunity to take the next set of lessons along the evolutionary ladder.

It can be powerful to contemplate the relationships in your life in the light of these themes. Every relationship contains its own package of karma. In some the karma runs strong and deep, in others it seems so thick it surrounds you at every turn. In other relationships the karma is light and easy. All karma has a certain quality to it. It is not the essence of the relationship, but it conceals the essence within the folds of its teachings.

Ironically, the most powerful relationships are not the easy ones, but those where the karma plays out the most intensely. Having said that, such relationships offer the greatest rewards, both in terms of inspiring self-love and as the deepest kinds of friendship.

In relationships, karma always equates with chemistry. The combining of two auras creates a third field that can be very powerful, and even at times overwhelming.

Karma also plays tricks on us innocent humans. Through the power of the Attractor Field and its themes of sexual chemistry, it magnetises us towards each other giving us a tantalising glimpse of our essence. Once we have been brought together, then like a great cosmic serpent, the karma begins to unravel and the story of our relationship begins. It doesn't take long for the Shadows to emerge. As we shall see, the depth of the Venus Sequence really concerns the patterns of our specific wounding through the Spheres known as the IQ, EQ, and SQ. Once the story begins to unravel our opportunity for inner growth becomes vast. To learn from an intimate relationship is perhaps the hardest and most rewarding of all spiritual paths.

KARMIC RELATIONSHIPS AS A NEW SPIRITUAL PATH

Although there are many new young shoots emerging in the world today, for the most part human relationships have never been seen as a spiritual path in their own right. In the Eastern and Middle Eastern mystical traditions, there has always been an emphasis on the path of Devotion, although this has often taken the form of devotion to a Godhead or guru. The fact is that there is very little traditional spiritual instruction in how to use one's relationships as a launch pad towards higher consciousness. The Venus Sequence offers us such guidance, and it also offers something else – it offers understanding. As you contemplate your Shadow patterns and their potential Gifts and Siddhis, you may begin to see a light at the end of the tunnel.

You really do not have to go any further than your front room to find the most viable, potent, and awesome spiritual path there has ever been.

The Venus Sequence invites you to make an enormous commitment. It asks you to place your primary relationship right at the centre of your inner life. It asks you to follow the storyline of its karma, and unpick the delicate weave of your own wounding from the drama.

It also asks you to be fiercely honest with yourself at a level you may never have considered before. As we have seen, karmic relationships contain great transformational power, but they are not for the faint of heart. This is a process that will bring you to your knees over and over again. You will have to go on surrendering to the karma, until you learn from it. This is a process that will take time. It will probably take you the rest of your life. But it will also offer you instant rewards, the greatest of which is the opening of your heart.

Most of us have had an experience of unconditional love. It may have been the first time we saw our child, or when we fell in love with a partner. However it came upon us, it lives inside us as more than just a memory. It is a cellular reference for who we truly are. Unconditional love places the needs of others before oneself. It is utterly unselfish and utterly humble. Whatever we long for in our outer life, a perfect home, a wonderful partner, a shiny new car, a thrilling new experience – it is all just a metaphor for our longing for our essence – for the state of unconditional love. Unless and until we rediscover our true open-hearted innocence, we will never stop longing for something or somewhere or someone.

If you are taken by this work, then the Venus Sequence invites you to give yourself one hundred percent to this contemplation on the nature of love through your relationships. It is also good to know that the Venus Sequence is not a wishy washy rose-tinted velour to drape around your shoulders. It is a gritty voyage into some uncharted and at times rather un-navigable inner waters!

You are not being asked to suddenly see your partner as a perfect sacred vessel of the Divine (even though they are). You are being asked to see the way you see your partner as nothing more than your own set of projections. To look inwardly into one's relationships like this takes some practise. It sometimes seems a thankless task. Each time you manage to see through your own projections, there is only you to pat yourself on the back. Often your partner will never know that you have just saved them from experiencing one of your Shadows! Because of this you will also need a good sense of humour on this path.

If you do feel drawn to this work, then please give it some time to soak into your life. To even begin to comprehend these patterns from the inside, rather than just at a mental level, you will need at least a year and probably a good deal more. You will be using your relationships as a mirror of your own ability to love. You will need perseverance, patience, and compassion, both for yourself and with your partner.

THE POWER OF ONE IN RELATIONSHIPS

There is a common assumption when beginning this kind of work that both partners need to be involved in the process. This is a misconception that often exacerbates even more tension in the relationship. The fact is that it only takes one person to transform a relationship. One aspect of karma is that although it binds two people together, the initial deep transformation work is often only tackled by one partner. If the teaching is correctly followed and embodied, then the other partner experiences a simultaneous opening. The moment you begin to disarm the Shadow patterns from ruling your reactions, you create a new kind of spaciousness in the relationship, and this is felt by your partner.

Knowing the above you do not have to include your partner in every aspect of your inner process. This can be a disturbance to them, especially if it does not feel like it is their path. This also helps you to keep the teaching moving inwardly instead of being caught in the common trap of always needing to process your own Shadows with your partner. If you feel the need to discuss the process with another (which is perfectly natural), it is often better to do so with a friend or mentor whose guidance you trust. Of course there are instances in which both partners in a relationship feel drawn to doing the inner work, and this can be a true blessing. You can use your inner victories to bolster each other's confidence, and you can give each other more space and understanding when you experience a Shadow pattern playing out through your behaviour or words.

The Venus Sequence is not a kind of primal therapy in which we are called to express every feeling in front of our partner. Neither is it about spending hours and hours processing our emotions together. The Venus Sequence is an interior path, a path of contemplation, in which you quietly observe your own behaviour reflected in the mirror of your partner. This does not mean for example, that if your partner is unpleasant to you that you are somehow to blame for their unpleasantness. It means that your response to their unpleasantness offers you a mirror for your own level of self love. You can always play back a scenario afterwards in your mind, and imagine how differently it might have played out had you been in a state of unconditional love.

In every situation you will need to hold unconditional love as your yardstick. This is not designed to make you feel bad about yourself. Very few people on this planet are able to maintain such a heightened state of frequency. But it can be used as a constant reminder that it is possible for you to attain such a state. This can be used as a great booster for your spirit.

Of course our relationships call us into intimacy with each other, so if your partner wants to know what is really going in inside you, they will always ask you. You must trust in that. If they do not ask, there is a good chance that they are not in a space to receive your current inner situation.

COURTESY – A TIMELESS VALUE

In our modern world we often overlook certain traditional values, which were once the mainstay of past generations. One of these is courtesy. It is often even referred to as 'common courtesy', even though it has become far from common in most modern relationships! Courtesy can be mistaken for formality and stuffiness, but in its pure form it has neither of these qualities. Courtesy is about basic human respect. When we get to know another person in an intimate relationship, we often forget to edit our Shadows or moods, as we would if we were with a stranger. Sometimes if you are feeling low, it is tempting to indulge your state in front of your partner.

Our usual reason for doing so is because we are unconsciously looking for love. However the effect this more often has on our partner is to make them feel low as well, since they would wish us to feel better.

Courtesy always considers the feelings of the other, and weighs them against our own. We do not have to conceal our feelings, but neither do we need indulge them. There are so many things that we show to our partner that simply would be better left inside. Courtesy maintains a very clean environment in a relationship. Neither does courtesy insist that our partner be courteous. We may have to lead this one by example. The net result of an increase in courteous behaviour is that your partner will feel better more of the time, and that in itself makes it a very precious quality to cultivate.

NORMALCY – MAINTAINING AN EVEN KEEL

As you begin to work with the layers of karma in your relationships, it's important to maintain the ordinary rhythms and routines of your life without creating too much disturbance. When we first become engaged in this kind of work, there is a tendency to try and do too much too quickly. It is a good idea not to expect too much of yourself. You do not have to suddenly behave differently or perfectly. That kind of sudden change is likely to be only of a surface quality. The Venus Sequence changes you gradually from the inside out. Likewise it may be a long time before you see changes reflected in your partner's behaviour. The Venus Sequence has more to do with recovery time – in other words, in how quickly you can catch yourself in a pattern, let it go, apologise if necessary, and move on.

This is the beauty of working with the Venus Sequence – that it teaches you from the inside out. It doesn't have to create any upheaval in your outer life, and you don't have to go out of the relationship in order to have an experience of a higher nature. If you cannot find it right here, right in the heart of your daily life, then it will never have a truly enduring quality.

KARMIC CLOSURE – NATURAL ENDINGS

As we have seen, every relationship has its own tapestry of karma. As we unravel the story and follow its lessons, sometimes the story comes to a natural conclusion. When one person begins to undergo a transformation, the partner in the relationship must also move through their own opening. If after considerable time this does not occur, then it usually means that the relationship is coming to a natural end. When this happens it will do so in a balanced way, without ill feeling. So often karmic relationships are brought to an end prematurely, because neither partner knows how to transform the Shadow patterns inwardly.

Natural endings usually bring sadness and are followed by periods of transition, but they can also be gratefully honoured for the experiences and lessons they have taught us. The advantage of staying with the karmic process is that if the relationship does end of its own accord even after much inner progress, then your attractor field will be ready to draw in an entirely new kind of relationship at a higher frequency than you have known before.

In a relationship that does not come to an end, there will still be mini-endings and new beginnings. Often these are marked by significant events such as moving home or a child being born or leaving school. As the karma of your relationship is followed and transformed, it becomes progressively lighter. Loving becomes more of an ongoing state regardless of the coming and goings of sadness and joy. The rewards of a long relationship in which the karma is continually burned off are truly vast. The final flowering of any relationship followed to its karmic conclusion is full-blown spiritual realisation through the embodiment of unconditional love.

BEING SINGLE

If you are single, the Venus Sequence is also a powerful tool of transformation. Your karma is always there playing out in your everyday life. You will have to be alert to the many opportunities that arise daily from your relationships with others. If you do not have a primary partner at your current stage in life, you can use all your other relationships as your means of transformation. Being alone has its own magic, and your Venus Sequence can become just as powerful an inner voyage as it is for someone in a relationship.

The advantage for you is that you do not have the distraction of another person's Shadows to continually test you.

This means that your own Shadows can be easy to see. You have an opportunity to dive very deeply into the Venus Stream. As you contemplate a certain Sphere, Gene Key, or line, you may note that it magically manifests in your outer life as some kind of a challenge. Embracing the challenge, you can then experience its hidden Gift.

As you explore your own Sequence and get in touch with these feelings, your journey can become deeply meditative. It can even become quite blissful. This is because you will experience a new level of Core Stability, and will throw out many old patterns. This will in turn revivify your Attractor Field, which may even draw in new relationships as you purify your consciousness. Whatever shape your journey with the Venus Sequence takes, there is as great an opportunity in being single as there is in being with someone. Regardless of your dharma - your destiny, the goal is always the same - the mining of the unconditional love that hides deep inside your DNA.

A NATURAL PAUSE

Before going any further into your Venus Sequence, there is a natural pause at this point in which follows important information concerning the ways in which our Shadow patterns are laid down during the cycles of our childhood. This section is of a mystical nature and unites many streams of wisdom, both ancient and contemporary. You are recommended to take your time in digesting and contemplating it before launching deeper into your Venus Sequence.

THE SACRED WOUND AND THE DOCTRINE OF THE SANSKARAS

A common thread to many of the world's creation stories is the notion of the sacred wound. This is the idea that every human being carries an aspect of suffering on behalf of the whole, and over the course of their lives as they learn to heal this wound through the lessons of love, so they bring healing to an aspect of the whole.

The Venus Sequence is a profound personal investigation into the sacred wound that you carry on behalf of the whole. It can show you the specific pattern and story of your deepest challenge in life, and it aids you in understanding it and healing it.

In the ancient Vedic traditions, there is a mysterious doctrine known as the 'sanskaras'. Traditionally your 'sanskaras' are seen as sense impressions or unconscious imprints left over from previous lives. In the Venus Sequence, we might view the sanskaras as a biogenetic sequence of codes that you inherited at the point of conception. As aspects of the sacred wound, your sanskaras are like a series of subtle memory slates stored inside your being, and each one refracts your view of life like a lens. Without your sanskaras, you would see life as it truly is, infinite and pure. However, your sanskaras skew your view of reality, making your life more challenging. Thus your sanskaras must be understood, purified, and transformed over the course of your life. This is their true purpose – to unlock the pathway to a higher consciousness, and to release the enormous healing capacity of the heart to love unconditionally.

Your Venus Sequence shows you the precise nature of your sanskaras as a sequence designed to be unlocked in a specific order. The Venus Sequence reveals to us how our sanskaras distort our awareness through the stages and cycles of our childhood. The unconscious patterns of the sacred wound are laid down in a sequence, and they can be unlocked and transformed in a sequence.

Each stage of your sequence therefore has a Gene Key and line that corresponds to it, and each of these Gene Keys carries a story about that phase of your childhood.

As you contemplate these Gene Keys and their themes in relation to your childhood, you may come to see the very forces that have shaped your life and relationships up to the present. This is a powerful journey that can bring about a profound inner healing.

AN INTRODUCTION TO THE 7-YEAR DEVELOPMENTAL CYCLES OF CHILDHOOD

From this point onwards in your Venus Sequence, you will be metaphorically travelling backwards in time through the various developmental phases of your childhood. We humans operate out of 7-year cellular cycles. Even though different cells are renewed at different rates, the majority of the cells inside the human body are replaced every 7 years. This is where your Hologenetic Profile becomes fascinating, because it gives you archetypal themes for each of the 3 main cycles from the point of your birth to the age of 21. As psychology has long known, our Shadow patterns are rooted in our childhood. However, what the Venus Sequence also shows us is how they are imprinted in our very DNA before we are even born.

CONCEPTION – THE INHERITANCE OF THE SACRED WOUND

Few moments in life are more magical than the point of conception. It is worth considering the depth of this moment at the beginning of your life. The sperm from your father and the ovum from your mother fuse together, mixing their respective genetic codes in a cosmic cocktail. This moment of fusion catalyses the evolution of a new set of patterns that in time becomes you. At the heart of your genesis lies this mysterious process known as the inheritance of the sacred wound.

At a cosmic level, the sacred wound is a rent or tear that formed right at the beginning of the universe, during the Big Bang. It is like a black hole of infinite density that can never be filled, and it is holographically encoded in every aspect of the universe. In essence, the sacred wound is the reason for our existence. Life itself is a response to the sacred wound – because as life tries to fill the mystical hole at the heart of creation, so evolution occurs.

When you were conceived, you received the living transmission of the sacred wound. Like the oak tree within the acorn, it was passed on through your ancestral DNA, and recombined in a unique way to form a series of patterns and pathways that will in time come to define who you are.

THE CORPUS CHRISTI AND THE INCARNATION OF THE TRINITY

Behind both the Venus Sequence and the Gene Keys lies a mystical body of teachings known as the Corpus Christi. This particular spiritual transmission is described in the 22nd Gene Key, and it concerns the mechanics of the invisible world that lies beyond our ordinary awareness. The Corpus Christi lays out a universe of 7 dimensions, each one holographically folded up inside each other like a series of Russian dolls. These dimensional fields can be seen as two pairs of trinities with the 7th dimension enfolding them all. Mystically speaking the sacred wound occurred when the trinities divided. In a human being the trinities are described as sheaths or bodies of different frequencies of consciousness. The lower trinity consists of the physical, astral (emotional), and mental bodies, whereas the upper trinity consists of the causal, buddhic, and atmic bodies.

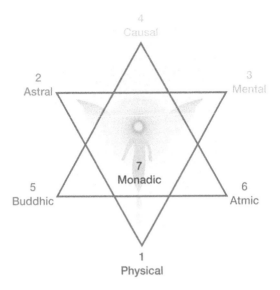

THE SEVEN SUBTLE BODIES OF THE CORPUS CHRISTI

The mythical fall of humankind is represented by this fundamental divide in our consciousness. Our lower nature reaches upwards through the current of evolution, and our higher nature reaches down into us through the current of involution. The sacred wound therefore drives us to search for our higher nature by reuniting the trinities, and experiencing our full Divine consciousness.

THE 3 TRIMESTERS OF PREGNANCY – THE UNWINDING OF THE WOUND

THE SACRED
WOUND: IMPRINTING
THROUGH THE 7-YEAR
CYCLES

CORE - 9 MONTHS GESTATION

SQ - AGE 0-7 (1ST TRIMESTER)

EQ - AGE 8-14 (2ND TRIMESTER)

IQ - AGE 15-21 (3RD TRIMESTER)

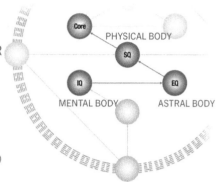

As we incarnate onto the physical plane, our separation from wholeness is played out in microcosmic form even while we are still in the womb. Each of the 3 trimesters of pregnancy relates to a dividing of our wholeness. Thus our physical body is imprinted with the sacred wound during the 1st Trimester, the astral (emotional) body is imprinted in the 2nd Trimester, and the mental body is imprinted in the 3rd Trimester. The nine months' process of gestation is thus a reenactment of the birth of the cosmos, as the trinity became imprinted at every level within the holographic universe.

This process of the division of our awareness during gestation should in no way be viewed in a negative light. It is the nature and wonder of our incarnative process as the sacred wound unwinds itself through the DNA helix, and creates the future storyline of our search for wholeness. In your Hologenetic Profile, your imprinting in the womb is represented by the Sphere of your Core Wound with its specific Gene Key and line.

BIRTH AND THE FIRST 7-YEAR CYCLE (0 –7 YRS)

The first seven years of our life are the foundation stone of who we are. The very moment we emerge from the womb is in itself a separation from wholeness. For the rest of our lives, we will unconsciously try and reconnect with this deep cellular memory of being unified with our mother. During this first 7-year cellular cycle our physical body is imprinted with the specific patterns (the sanskaras) that will unconsciously dominate much of our lives. At the Shadow frequency, we each have a deep fear pattern that is layered down during this first cycle. Out of this Shadow however also emerges our SQ – our Spiritual Quotient. Your SQ is a measure of the level that you allow spiritual intelligence to animate your life. As you embrace the Shadow of this Gene Key, so you unlock the Gifts of your SQ, which will in turn guide your life.

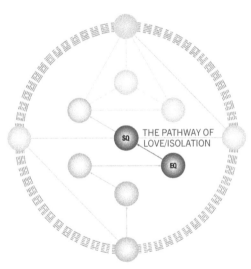

SQ: THE FIRST SEVEN YEARS (0-7)

In your Hologenetic Profile, your contemplation allows you to reach deeply into these patterns through an understanding of the Sphere of your SQ and the Pathway of Realisation.

As the deepest level of your Venus Sequence, when you awaken your SQ to its full potential, you will experience a complete reawakening of your highest consciousness.

THE ASTRAL BODY, PUBERTY, AND THE SECOND 7-YEAR CYCLE (8 – 14 YRS)

The second 7-year cycle of our life is the phase in which we move through puberty, and develop our primary emotional patterns. In esoteric terms this phase relates to the full incarnation of our astral body, that aspect of our nature that relates primarily through our emotions and desires. It is during this cycle that our astral sanskaras are imprinted as a series of emotional defence strategies designed to protect our heart from pain. These emotional Shadow patterns then follow us into adulthood, where they become ingrained as repeating emotional issues that undermine our relationships. Out of these Shadow patterns emerges our EQ – our Emotional Quotient. Your EQ is a measure of the level of your emotional maturity – that is, your ability to take responsibility for your own Shadow patterns and your level of emotional empathy. As you embrace the Shadow of the Gene Key of your EQ, you will find your relationships are gradually transformed.

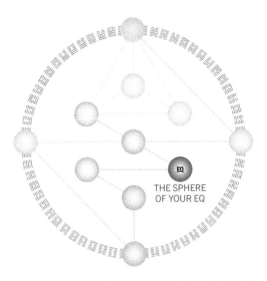

EQ: THE SECOND SEVEN YEARS (8-14)

In your Hologenetic Profile, your contemplation of the Sphere of your EQ and the Pathway of Love can bring about a permanent opening of your heart through an ongoing process of self-forgiveness, leading to an experience of unconditional love.

THE MENTAL BODY AND THE THIRD 7-YEAR CYCLE (15 – 21 YRS)

The third 7-year cycle of our life takes us through our teenage years into young adulthood. These are the formative years of our thinking life. In this cycle we form our primary mental views of life – our opinions, our beliefs, and our basic psychology. Our mental view of the world is founded upon our earlier emotional imprinting in our second 7 year-cycle, which in turn is built upon the basic physiological patterns we developed in our first 7 year cycle. Thus our IQ emerges from our EQ, which is rooted in our SQ! The further we go back, the deeper the roots of our Shadows are found.

Your IQ is a measure of your mental intelligence – your ability to use both sides of your brain and to think with flexibility and vision. At the same time, the Shadow of the Gene Key relating to your IQ gives rise to unconscious mental patterns and views rooted in a lack of self-worth. As you dismantle the patterns of this Shadow in your own mind, so you will find that the communication in all your relationships becomes much easier and clearer.

IQ: THE THIRD SEVEN YEARS (15-21)

In your Hologenetic Profile, your contemplation of the Sphere of your IQ and the Pathway of Intelligence will catalyse a process in which your mind opens up to a whole new level of insight and living wisdom.

THE VENUS SEQUENCE –
UNPICKING THE WEAVE OF THE WOUND

The purpose of the Venus Sequence is to bring awareness to this complex process in which your Shadow patterns were laid down through your childhood. Because the sacred wound consists of these layers of wounding (the sanskaras) that were imprinted in a chronological sequence, by following that sequence in reverse, we can essentially unpick the weave of the wound.

It is rather like removing the layers of an onion, although the surprise is that each layer contains a Gift. The whole process is a deep psychological journey where our contemplation is trained on each of the stages for a period of time.

There are no rules in how you apply the Venus Sequence to your life. The challenge and the beauty of contemplation is that you will have to find your own way. If you wish to seek support in moving through this process then that is fine. You must give yourself whatever you need. The other thing to realise is that when you place your awareness on an issue that is buried inside you, that issue will tend to rise up and manifest. This is a great opportunity for you to parent yourself, and move through a transformation. The most important aspect of this work is to follow the sequence itself step by step. You will find your own rhythm of contemplation. Some people like to move through the whole sequence lightly, taking it in, first of all at an intellectual level. Then they may go back to the beginning, and do it again in greater depth. Other people may wish to move slowly through each step, waiting until some form of insight has occurred that allows them to move on to the next step.

The whole Venus process is like unpicking an intricate weave, with sections of knotting that require painstaking attention. Remember it is your life that will be your muse, so pay attention to your relationships, to your moods, to your modes of thinking, and to your physical impulses. Above all, teach yourself to take responsibility for what goes on inside your being, rather than projecting it out onto others as blame. The Venus Sequence is first and foremost about personal accountability.

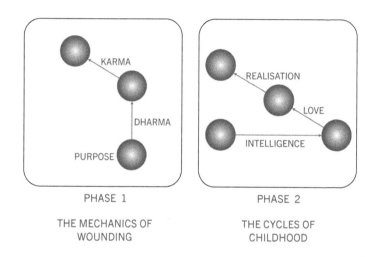

PHASE 1

THE MECHANICS OF
WOUNDING

PHASE 2

THE CYCLES OF
CHILDHOOD

THE TWO PHASES OF THE VENUS SEQUENCE

6. THE SPHERE OF YOUR IQ

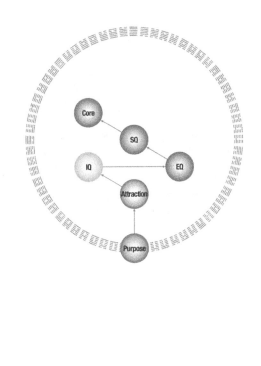

THE SPHERE OF YOUR IQ –
THE WONDER OF THE TEENAGE MIND

When we arrive at the Sphere of your IQ, we begin our journey backwards in time from young adulthood through our years as a teenager. This part of your journey concerns the cycle of imprinting between the ages of 14 and 21. This 3rd seven-year cycle is an intense period in the life of anyone, both as a parent and as a child. If you happen to be a parent as you contemplate this section, it may greatly help you to understand the teenage cycle of your child, as he or she makes the delicate transition into early adulthood. As a parent, one of the most important things to know is that we cannot prevent our child from experiencing their own version of the sacred wound. Particularly during this 3rd phase when our children come into fuller contact with the wider world, we must learn to let them have their experiences. The most we can do is establish basic boundaries and stand in our own Core Stability, so that they can rely on us for wisdom and compassion.

The other vital factor in understanding the Venus Sequence is that it is about the child inside you. During this phase you may see patterns and aspects of behaviour left over from your years as a teenager, but that still remain in your psyche. Seeing yourself as a multi-layered, multi-aged human being can be very revealing. The idea that we can continually integrate our childhood even as we age is what leads to a very fulsome life. There are gifts we had as teenagers that we may have forgotten – for instance, our incredibly dextrous mind and its ability to absorb information across many dimensions. Many sharp minds soon become over-intellectualised, losing their sense of 'springiness' and edge. The budding teenage brain is a hive of neural possibility, unclouded by dogma, belief system, and opinion.

As your contemplation moves into this cycle of your growth, you may discover places in your mind where thinking has become bogged down, where the natural optimism of youthful experimental thinking has lost its crystal sheen.

You should prepare yourself for a mental reckoning – for an honest laser-like scan of the way your thinking has developed over the years since you were a child. This first part of the Venus Sequence offers us a powerful opportunity to unlock a revolutionary positivity whose source is in our minds.

INTERNAL ARCHITECTURE - SURFING THE SUBTLE PLANES

It is during our teen years that our mind sets the tone of the way we will think for most of our lives. Much depends on our social milieu, the quality of parenting we receive, the nature of our family life and our friends, teachers, and peers. In short, our minds are forged out of our early relationships. Sometimes our mind will rebel in a certain direction because of a strong emotional reaction to an authority figure. At other times our mind will be moulded and shaped by a powerful belief system that we are drawn into. The most fortunate among us will develop our minds in a certain direction in response to an inspirational and open-hearted mentor figure or teacher of some kind.

It will be interesting for you to begin a contemplative journey into the relationships that most strongly influenced your mind between the ages of 14 and 21. You can examine the major influences in your life at this time – both from your social peer group, your family, and through your education. Which subjects at school most captivated you? Which teachers caught your imagination? Which if any family members influenced your mind, either as an inspiration or a reaction? You might like to create a mental tree of the influential relationships you had during this phase of your life.

When you do this in depth, you may begin to see how your mind developed in a particular direction. The revelation of the Venus Sequence is built upon the existence of subtle planes of being that lie outside the 'normal' capacities of our logical mind. These planes of being interlock with each other, but can also be graded at different levels of frequency in order that we can better understand them.

At the densest level is the physical plane, where our bodies feed us sensory information from our physical environment. At the next level up lies the astral plane – the realm of emotions and desires. Most of us have been taught that emotions are the by-products of physical chemistry, so the idea of emotions coming from another plane altogether can really open up our minds to new ways of thinking and seeing. In the Venus Sequence, we also look at life from the other direction – we contemplate the idea that it is our emotional life that informs and creates our physical chemistry.

In the above scenario we might well ask the question: where do emotions come from? Can we open up to the possibility that they are frequencies that we actually attract into our aura? When we look at life in this way, it makes us feel far more empowered. We no longer need think of ourselves as victims of our chemistry. Indeed, now we can become the architects of our chemistry. In this scenario a heightened positive attitude would draw high frequency emotional impulses into our aura, which would then impact our chemistry through our endocrine system. On the other hand, a pessimistic 'victim' attitude would magnetise low frequency impulses into our aura making us feel sluggish and depressed. This notion of frequency is so important that it underpins the entire Gene Keys Synthesis. It opens us up to the possibility that the universe is magical – a possibility we may well have once embraced during our early years.

Let us then extend this concept of the subtle planes of being still further into the domain of our minds. If emotions exist on a subtle plane of their own with a whole spectrum of frequencies, ranging from coarse negative emotions to refined and elevated emotions, then the same may be true of thinking. This brings us to the next subtle plane – the mental plane. The mental plane exists at an even subtler plane than the astral plane. Again, we have been trained to think of thoughts and thinking as originating in our brain, but what if our brain is simply the machinery that processes information drawn in from the quantum field? This means that thoughts may also exist as frequencies or energy signatures that live in another dimension.

Again, if we hold a positive mental attitude and an open mind, then we would magnetise mental frequencies that form in our brain as inspirational thinking. On the other hand, at the Shadow frequency, a pessimistic, over-opinionated mindset would limit the capacities of our brain, and thus lower our IQ and our intelligence.

This way of looking at the inner architecture of our lives can liberate us from an old paradigm that was based on the idea that consciousness is a by-product of the physical organism. This kind of thinking has dominated in our modern scientific age, and although science has consequently made huge leaps and bounds in its discoveries, the price has been high. We have neglected an entire worldview that is more holistic in origin.

Interestingly enough, as science stretches itself further, it finds itself returning to a more multi-dimensional view based on the possible existence of dimensions and planes of reality that lies beyond our senses. One of the hallmarks of our teenage cycle of development is a powerful attraction and openness to the genre of science fiction and fantasy. These genres allow the mind its fullest capacity to stretch out into realms and possibilities that we can only access through the power of imagination and intuition.

EXORCISING THE MENTAL BODY

One of the things that happens to us during our 3rd 7-year cycle of development is that our minds receive the imprint of the sacred wound as it moves up the planes of our being from our earlier cycles. We have seen how the wound itself is received at conception, then imprinted during the three trimesters of gestation to be made manifest later in our three 7-year developmental cycles. Because the mental wound is the last aspect to develop (in the 3rd trimester), it is the first aspect we must tackle, if we are to move any deeper in our healing process. This is why we begin our deeper process of contemplation here.

Just as there is a subtle mental plane, so we might extend our thinking even further to encompass the idea that we also have a mental body. This allows us a broader conception of how we build up our thinking process throughout our lives.

It might also be helpful to see the mental body as a subtle bioenergetic sheath that extends throughout our aura. As we have seen, during our teenage cycle, we have a natural affinity for the supernatural, and our mental body is vast, extending out far into the holographic cosmos. As we get older our thinking tends to undergo a closing down, and thus our mental body shrinks and contracts to encompass only as much as we allow it to.

During our 2nd 7-year cycle in which the sacred wound is imprinted through our astral (emotional) body, we experience an emotional contraction as we learn our primary emotional defence strategies for coping with the pain of the world. This in turn is then transferred to our mental body during this 3rd teenage cycle. This time however the contraction is mental. Although the wound may be emotional in origin, it then closes off aspects of the mind. Thus we establish an unconscious pattern of thinking whose purpose is to protect us from hurt. At the same time, this deep fear creates an undercurrent to our thinking which prevents us from seeing life as it is, without judgement. In the Venus Sequence, this pattern is represented by the Sphere of your IQ and its specific Gene Key and line.

As we examine the way in which we think about ourselves, we will see how it influences the way we think about others, and therefore the way in which we relate. The Sphere of your IQ really represents a blind-spot in your psyche. Once you begin to see this pattern, you can begin the process of dismantling it through awareness. This is really a kind of mental exorcism, as we throw out old unconscious belief patterns that keep us from relating with the world in an open-hearted way. As you go about this extraordinary subtle process, you can really contemplate how you have allowed the way you see the world to be compromised. This is a process that will take some time, and that will continue throughout your journey along the Golden Path.

REACTION AND IGNITION – TRIGGERS AND SPARKS

There are specific junctions along the Golden Path where a great deal of dynamic force is held under pressure by our conditioning. This makes the Shadow issues there more intense, but also provides us with an opportunity to catalyse swift transformation. Three Spheres in particular have this quality – the Sphere of Evolution, the Sphere of IQ, and the Sphere of our Culture. Each of these Spheres acts like a trigger in our psyche, so that as we train our awareness on the issues it represents, we may open a floodgate inside us.

As was mentioned earlier, the Venus Stream - the actual living transmission of awakening energy behind the Venus Sequence – follows a watery allegory. As the currents of the Venus Stream flow along the Pathway of Karma, they pierce the Sphere of the IQ like a sharp jet of water travelling under pressure – rather like an underground geyser erupting to the surface.

The Sphere of your IQ represents a mental pattern that holds back the pressure of emotion deep within the cells of your body. This is why in relationships we can be so easily triggered by certain issues, people, or vocal tones. Whenever a low frequency emotional pattern is triggered by another person, there you can see this pattern at work.

It is intriguing and perhaps shocking to realise how the mental patterns we formed as a teenager still persist inside us as mature adults. Many of us never reach a fuller mental or emotional maturity for the rest of our lives. It takes a lot of courage to take responsibility for one's own Shadow patterns. What this means is that when we experience an emotional conflict with a partner, what is often occurring is that two childhood patterns are fighting against each other. Without awareness, such patterns can be very painful and may seem relentless.

It is very important and worthwhile to dig deeply into the Sphere of your IQ and the Gene Key that corresponds to it. This is a place to put your full attention. It is also a good idea to travel back in your memory, and rekindle some of the major events that marked out your teenage years. The events we remember most easily are memorable for a good reason, so they are a good place to begin our contemplation. Often when we bring our attention to a specific set of memories, then the cells that carry those memories release other connected memories. Remember, contemplation involves more than just thinking about something. It is a living re-enactment of the patterns themselves. As you bring them to light, so your awareness can see them clearly for what they are – triggers that set off highly charged emotional issues.

The huge benefit of doing this inner work is that awareness changes everything. Instead of being a victim of a reaction pattern, your new mindset ignites a deep cellular healing process. As you change the way you think about yourself and others, so your emotions begin to travel more freely through your astral body. This process is discussed in more depth as we enter the Pathway of Intelligence. The important thing to realise is that the same energy that made us react also ignites our healing.

THE SHADOW

It is interesting that in order to unlock the deeper currents of our emotions, we must first unlock our minds. The Shadow of your IQ tells the same story in every human being – just in different ways. The common story is that at some point we began to believe ourselves unworthy of love. Out of this deep-seated belief, we developed a narrow way of thinking and behaving that often only emerges when we feel emotionally threatened or uncomfortable. When you contemplate this Shadow, look at the way you behave when you feel stressed or under pressure. See how your mind contracts around the emotions that lie beneath the behaviour. It is important to get in touch with the teenager inside you and their feelings.

The Shadow of your IQ is a pattern that you developed whenever you felt overwhelmed by the power of your emotions. Try and see how this Gene Key and its line holds an incredible key for you. When you can see the power this pattern has over you, then you will open up the floodgates to a deeper process of cellular healing that may go on for some time. As a trigger in your psyche, this Shadow should be approached with an open mind and given as much time to unfold as it needs.

THE GIFT

The Gifts of our IQ are manifold. Once our mind has been freed from holding back our fuller maturity, an enormous amount of energy is released through our body and brain. Having said this, neural pathways take some rewiring.

We will have to be continually alert for the Shadow pattern whenever we experience emotional discomfort. However, the great news is that as you open your mind once again to the possibility that you are worthy of love, then you become more intelligent! Your IQ represents your mental alacrity, but it also involves something else that is not a part of the average IQ test – optimism. Optimism is not the same as positive thinking, which can be natural or forced as a technique. Optimism comes from drawing in high frequency thought forms. It is the nature of a true open mind. The Gift of your IQ is therefore more than just being clever or intellectual – it is about open-circuit thinking. The mark of true intelligence is the certainty that you are fully worthy of love. When you consider the Gene Key of your IQ, see which qualities shine through you when you live with this kind of a loving, accepting, and forgiving open mind.

THE SIDDHI

The Siddhi of your IQ allows you access to the quantum field of the whole universe. The mental plane can only take your consciousness so far, for there is an awareness system in your body that allows you to transcend the limits of your thinking. This involves the subtler bodies that lie beyond the mental body.

The mental body has a higher counterpart known as the Atmic body, and this allows you to experience a depth of consciousness that is far, far beyond the mind. The Atmic body can only relay Truth, and it does so through silence, once the mind has fallen silent. When the Venus Sequence has been ignited inside your DNA, the expansion of your consciousness will continue on its own.

The trigger point of the Sphere of your IQ goes on unlocking energy through your being, and the wider your mind opens, the more love comes pouring through your heart. You should therefore take the Siddhi of your IQ seriously.

When you examine the Shadow of your IQ, see what manner of vastness it is holding back inside you, and hold this quality always in your heart.

THE 6 LINES OF YOUR IQ

Each of the 6 lines of your IQ represent a different kind of psychological bias. These are generalised modes or styles of thinking that underpin our behaviour. You will also see that each line has a Shadow keynote. This relates to a pattern of thinking and behaviour that we developed between the age of 14 and 21.

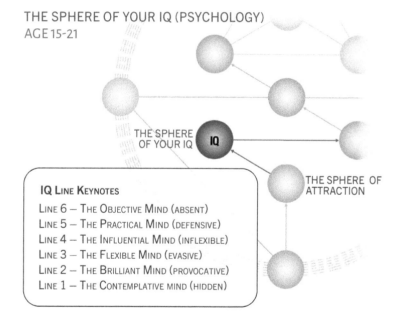

THE SPHERE OF YOUR IQ (PSYCHOLOGY)
AGE 15-21

THE SPHERE OF YOUR IQ   IQ

THE SPHERE OF ATTRACTION

IQ Line Keynotes

Line 6 — The Objective Mind (absent)
Line 5 — The Practical Mind (defensive)
Line 4 — The Influential Mind (inflexible)
Line 3 — The Flexible Mind (evasive)
Line 2 — The Brilliant Mind (provocative)
Line 1 — The Contemplative mind (hidden)

Line 1: The Contemplative Mind (hidden)

The foundation of all mental genius is the ability to contemplate. You may well think that contemplation is something that anyone can do, but this is not always the case. Contemplation takes discipline and open-mindedness. The contemplative mind also underpins a contemplative lifestyle, so if you have a 1st line IQ then this kind of lifestyle will suit you very well. You need plenty of time to peruse. You need regular breaks throughout your day in order for insight to percolate. Contemplation is a way of being. It is easy-going and rhythmical, and enjoys a kind of meandering lifestyle in which there is a consistent blend of interior focus and exploration. A person with a 1st line IQ will be one of the most fascinating people you will ever encounter. Because of their internal focus, you may not even realise how deep such a person is.

There have always been contemplative types living among us. In times gone by, these people of the 1st line IQ might have taken refuge in the great religious traditions, or they would have become our wise ones. Contemplation thrives on aloneness, so if you have a 1st line IQ then those around you need to understand this genetic imperative that drives you. This does not mean that you have to keep going away to be alone – it means that you carry your aloneness around inside you. It is a palpable inner force, carrying with it great love and patience.

At the Shadow frequency however, this kind of psychology is very uncomfortable, both for you and for others. The 1st line has a natural tendency towards turning inwards. As a teenager, you may well have dealt with pain and intense emotion by turning inwards and withdrawing into your mind. This is the hidden mind. No one ever knows what is going on inside a child like this. They may physically lock themselves in their bedroom, or they may just clam up and tell you nothing.

If you have a 1st line IQ, then you need to learn to find a way to safely express what is going on inside you. This does not always have to be through spoken words. There are many levels of communication available to the contemplative mind.

Sometimes a poem, a picture, a smile, a touch, or a clear action can say far more about our inner state than any spoken word. Later in life the Shadow of the 1st line IQ can make such people very difficult to get to know, as their feelings may have become so habitually internalised that they are difficult to access. If you have a 1st line IQ, then anything that helps you towards a greater self expression will be hugely beneficial for you and for the world.

Line 2: The Brilliant Mind (Provocative)

When our IQ is refracted through the 2nd line theme, it literally shines out with the beauty of its genius. This is a mind that is always surprising, as it is always making quantum leaps. The brilliance of the 2nd line truly comes alive in this Sphere. These kinds of minds are the great voyagers of the mental plane. They will take human thinking right to the edge of its capability.

This is thinking that combines both left brain logic with right brain vision. Such minds are often seen as far ahead of the age they live through. These are inventive minds that often lead pioneering breakthroughs. They may appear in almost any domain of human endeavour from the sciences to the arts and music. The 2nd line mind is not just about thinking – it presupposes a highly expressive and creative life. These are people designed to catch the limelight.

At the Shadow frequency, the 2nd line is all provocation. It is simply unable to hold back its anger and resentment. These are the kinds of teenagers who are often seen as highly rebellious and even obnoxious. They will strike out when they feel threatened or vulnerable, or if they do not strike out at another, they will take it out on themselves in some way.

They rail against the fates, and are often deeply misunderstood by others. Of all the lines, the 2nd line IQ is most likely to be unjustly punished for their behaviour.

Even later in life this pattern will still persist at difficult moments. In an adult, this may manifest as a tendency to explode in fits of rage that do not seem in any way matched to the issue at hand.

The 2nd line must therefore learn to manage their anger on the surface, but more importantly they must understand where this pattern stems from. In most cases it comes as a reaction to a feeling of being deeply misunderstood by others. This feeling cuts so deep that it becomes an assumption that is projected onto anyone the moment that emotions begin to run high. The secret of this 2nd line is therefore to realise that it is not others who are responsible for your feelings, but you alone. The maturing of this realisation can lead to a reframing of the pattern, which can then find a new and healthy creative outlet in the world.

Line 3: The Flexible Mind (Evasive)

The 3rd line pattern is founded upon its flexibility. This is a mindset that thinks on its feet. The beauty of the 3rd line is the sheer scope of its knowledge. We should remember that we are looking here at mental belief systems that affect our relationships. The 3rd line pattern is a mind that explores all kinds of belief systems and mental structures. This is what makes it so versatile, and eventually can lead to a real gift for communicating with and listening to others. If you have a 3rd line IQ, then others will always feel understood and accepted by you. You will have the ability to think sympathetically, which can lead to all kinds of possibilities. The 3rd line mind is also invaluable in strategic thinking – because it is so absorbent it can help others in all kinds of ways. It may also have an unusual memory with the ability to access all kinds of weird and wonderful data when needed.

The Shadow of the 3rd line pattern is about being evasive. These can be people who never give a straight answer to a question. This is a mental pattern that has learned to avoid the real issue by becoming adept at deflecting attention away from itself. Being evasive can also take many forms. During the teenage years, this is often a tendency to get easily bored and lose interest in things, for instance in school work. It can be a painful thing for a parent to witness their child seemingly throwing away the golden opportunity of their potential during this challenging cycle of life. One must remember that there is no fault in these kinds of patterns.

The 3rd line always bounces back, so long as it is given the right mix of firm boundaries and creative understanding. In later relationships, the 3rd line may however continue to find it challenging to relate with others because of this earlier pattern. The key as ever is awareness. Awareness of the pattern frees us from being a victim of the pattern. Then it becomes something we can work with in a creative way.

Line 4: The Influential Mind (Inflexible)

If you have a 4th line IQ, then you are born to be influential. Unlike the 3rd line with its changing viewpoint, the 4th line tends to pursue things in a straight line, with unwavering focus and dedication. These are people who often find a single arena that they love, and then they become masters of that arena. When we look around at the most influential people in the world, or in history, we often see that they are people who devoted their energy and attention towards a single goal within a single field of endeavour. This is what is required in order to arrive at a breakthrough. The 4th line also has the skill of communication. They not only have a great idea, they also have the means to convey it clearly to others. You can see the recipe for influence here. The 4th line IQ is a person that can use the mind as a means to relate more clearly and precisely and with genuine warmth and heartfulness.

When it comes to the Shadows, we always see how our potential strengths become the very blind spot that keeps us trapped in a repeating low frequency pattern. Until we understand and see the pattern, we will never dismantle it. Here in the 4th line, we see inflexibility – the inability or unwillingness to bend our viewpoint to accommodate another person's views or feelings.

As a pattern developed during our teenage cycle, this can become an entrenched belief or set of opinions about others or the world that attempts to keep us from feeling a deeper pain. Often with the 4th line the opinion is projected onto another (usually a parent). This can make it very difficult to communicate with the child or young adult. As with each of the 6 lines of the IQ, the pattern is rooted in a deep sense of our own unworthiness.

Because we do not feel worthy of love, we project this onto those closest to us. In later life the 4th line can feel increasingly isolated, unless they can come to terms with the feelings lying beneath their mind. The 4th line pattern is very difficult to dislodge if one tries to tackle it through the mind. It is often better to bypass the mind altogether, and either work directly with the pattern at an emotional level or even directly with the physical body.

Line 5: The Practical Mind (Defensive)

In our journey along the Golden Path, we have seen the 5th line as a great problem solver, a fixer, and a self-empowered leader. If you have a 5th line IQ, then you are a catalyst for dynamic change and transformation. This is the kind of mind that can always sift through the haystack and within seconds locate the needle. The 5th line has an inherent ability to organise information in such a way that it is understood by anyone and everyone. The 5th line makes the complex accessible, bringing clarity to seemingly impenetrable issues. It sees both depth and detail and it doesn't waste time or energy in flowery expression, but loves to bring things right down to their essence.

Because of the above qualities, the 5th line has always been sought out by others for guidance, or looked to for leadership and inspiration. When things get difficult or challenging in life, we all need the loving but penetrating wisdom of the 5th line.

So many people never get to live out the wonderful potential of their higher purpose in life, because a part of them never grows up. The mental patterns we develop as teenagers often stay with us for the rest of our lives, unless we go through some kind of a life affirming crisis or awakening. The 5th line undermines itself by becoming a victim of its own self-pity. These are teenagers who fall into such a deep funk inside themselves, often convincing themselves that everyone is against them. This belief puts them constantly on the defence, making it very difficult for them to trust anyone who comes close. Once again, later in life this is a pattern that will persist whenever one feels under threat, emotionally or otherwise.

And once again, this pattern can only be broken by self awareness. In the case of the 5th line, the self awareness must be taken in very deeply, because their mind can be so clever. The 5th line IQ can also be overly intellectual, and can slide easily into a cynical arrogance. The dismantling of such patterns can require a complete gestalt shift for the 5th line – a process that is never easy, but is always very humbling and empowering.

Line 6: The Objective Mind (Absent)

The 6th line IQ is the only one of the 6 lines that can call itself wholly objective. Each of the other lines carries an agenda. At the higher frequencies, an agenda can be beneficial, for example like an urge to be of service, whereas at the low frequencies it is always self-serving. The 6th line however, is designed to surf the mental plane without agenda, although getting to this stage may be a drawn-out process.

On the way to achieving no agenda, the 6th line mind may well develop various viewpoints. Each view in turn will be dropped or transcended, until a higher view arises that can see things for what they are, without adding anything on top. The mind that sees in this way is rare indeed.

To see things for what they are is the hallmark of a truly enlightened mind. It is the sign of a silent mind. This is the radical potential of the 6th line IQ. If you have this in your profile, then you will most probably lead an interesting life. You may live many lives within a single life until you finally arrive at your zenith – a place where IQ can no longer be measured and genius can no longer be quantified. In its most natural form the 6th line mind reflects nature. Like the I Ching, it will mirror the terrestrial and celestial patterns of the ever changing present. Out of this inner alignment can pour forth the voice of a wild, living wisdom, an objective wisdom that is the voice of nature itself.

The Shadow version of the 6th line IQ is expressed through a sense of absence. There is a sense in some teenagers of a vital aspect of their self-expression simply being absent.

The eyes lose their lustre, a kind of torpor seems to have a hold of their minds. In some respects they appear to be disincarnate, disinterested, and disrespectful of everything. When this pattern persists in our relationships later on in life, then at times it may seem as though you become completely numb to emotions.

The 6th line often thinks it has something wrong with it. This sense of absence that grips the mental body will also freeze the emotions tightly around the heart, choking the life force. To heal such a deep pattern, you must be very patient with yourself, and you will also need a patient partner. When your heart suddenly goes cold, it is a memory in the cells that has been triggered. It is not your fault. You simply have to be with the pattern, wrapping it in your awareness, knowing that it cannot survive so long as you bring your attention to it. If you wait, then sure enough a shift will occur, your heart will spontaneously re-engage when it feels ready. Over time this will happen more readily and more quickly.

CONTEMPLATING THE SPHERE OF YOUR IQ

Having digested the 6 lines of the IQ, you may need some time to take in this Sphere, your Gene Key, and how it all works inside you. Earlier on in this work we spoke of the three different types of Contemplation – mental, emotional, and physical. When you contemplate the Sphere of your IQ, you are engaging the subtlest of these – the mental plane. Contemplation through your mental body often begins with doubt or confusion. Certainly it begins with not knowing. And then you begin to think over the subject – you need to think about it in a sustained but unserious way. If you get too serious, then you will go into a kind of mental contraction which will feel very uncomfortable.

We have seen that the allegory of water likens the Sphere of our IQ to the power of water to pierce rock. You can use the sharpness of your intellect to help you pierce the emotional Shadow patterns that sometimes possess you. Part of the intellectual world-view that you formed in your teenage cycle will be based upon an unconscious notion of your own unworthiness. Use your newborn insight to deflate this world view!

To contemplate the Sphere of your IQ, you will also have to cultivate a love of mystery. There are issues inside you that began as a teenager, and they remain unresolved to this day. You needn't rush to be rid of them. Our healing is about entertaining all aspects of our Self, so you can invite the young adult inside you to be with you. Look at yourself and how you were during this time period. Think about those people you know at that age right now. Can you determine which of the 6 patterns they seem to be manifesting? You needn't rush out and find out anyone's time of birth – these patterns are there in everyone. Once you begin to listen and become familiar with the 6 lines and their themes, you will see them everywhere.

The beauty of the Venus Stream is that it is self-healing and self-revealing. Self-illumination is an unfathomable process that sneaks up on you as you learn how to contemplate.

At the mental level, your mental body will begin to expand as you draw in more refined currents and thought forms from the mental plane. We live inside a holographic matrix, and insights occur whenever we pierce one of the veils between the many dimensions that make up our greater self. Remember that the Venus Stream at this stage in our process is like an underground geyser bursting forth from the inner planes. So long as we give ourselves the right environment of compassion, patience, and inquiry, eventually we will experience the mystery of self illumination.

7. THE PATHWAY OF INTELLIGENCE

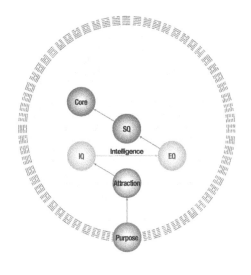

THE PATHWAY OF INTELLIGENCE

When we were introduced to the Activation Sequence, we saw a very simple threefold pattern that is universal in its nature – we are confronted with a challenge, and it is our wholehearted response to this challenge that allows us to experience a breakthrough. As we incorporate the breakthrough into our life, so we strengthen our core stability. These three phases – Challenge, Breakthrough, and Core Stability are a motif that continues throughout the Golden Path. As we approach the sixth Pathway - the Pathway of Intelligence - we arrive at another kind of challenge. This time the challenge is not about our Life's Work or our outer life. It is a far deeper challenge, because it underpins the challenge of our Life's Work and Evolution.

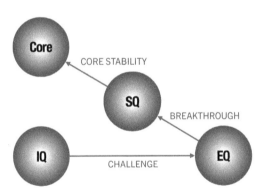

EMOTIONAL CHALLENGE

The challenge of the Pathway of Intelligence concerns the correct balance of the mind and the emotions in your life. A healthy equilibrium between these two planes is a major indicator of true intelligence. We have already seen through the Sphere of the IQ how powerful the mind can be at holding back the emotions. The Venus Sequence is all about emotion. Its purpose is to free the emotions, so that they flow through us effortlessly as nature intended.

However, the challenge is always about finding the balance. If your mind dominates over your feelings then your life force is stymied, whereas if your emotions run amok to the detriment of your mental state, your nervous system will pay a high price, not to mention your relationships.

The Venus Sequence teaches us that intelligence is a process rather than an achievement or birthright. This process moreover is intimately linked to our awakening. In our relationships the gauge of our awakening is our ability to communicate clearly, openly, and with respect. This Pathway of Intelligence is therefore all about balanced and open communication, which lies at the heart of our ability to relate with others. It is interesting that we so often view intelligence as an individual phenomenon. Through the lens of the Venus Sequence however, you may come to view intelligence as an interactive forcefield that lies between two or more living auras. This is the deeper meaning of the Pathway of Intelligence. Every relationship actually has a natural intelligence of its own, and when we find the keys to unlock this intelligence, then we will have triggered an extraordinary process of collaborative awakening that is only now just emerging in our world.

THE EDEN LOOP

We may note that every Pathway comprising the Venus Sequence has a Shadow keynote (with the exception of the final Pathway of Realisation). In this case it is the Pathway of Defence. The two Spheres at either end of this Pathway of Intelligence and Defence dictate the quality and frequency of our communication. If our low frequency mental teenage pattern (IQ) is in charge, then this will most likely trigger the other person's emotional defence strategy (EQ). This in turn triggers our own low frequency IQ pattern to engage. In the Venus Sequence, this process of the sequential triggering of each other's childhood patterns is known as the 'Eden Loop'. The Eden Loop is a low frequency biofeedback loop that often occurs in relationships as two people's Shadow sequences collide. A major part of working with the Venus Sequence concerns the awareness of such patterns that prevent us from communicating in an open and respectful way.

SHADOW THEMES

Once awareness enters into the equation, we are more likely to catch our own reactive shadow patterns as they are occurring. In this way we can prevent ourselves from being a victim of those patterns. This is why it was stated earlier, that it only takes one person to begin the transformation of a relationship. The moment one person refuses to engage their side of the Eden Loop, then the pattern itself has nowhere to go. The Eden aspect only emerges as this Pathway begins to open up between two people. The Shadow is transformed into a loving state, and a much deeper form of communication becomes possible. In order to understand how the Pathway of Intelligence really works in your own relationships, you need to become more and more aware of how you communicate, and of how you react to the way others communicate.

How then do we break out of this Eden Loop? Is simple awareness of the pattern really enough? Is there anything else we can do to unlock this intriguing forcefield of intelligence hiding in our relationships? The answer to these questions lies in a very simple technique described below. You can begin applying this technique to all and any of your relationships.

THE ART OF JOINING

The following technique is adapted from the work of Don and Martha Rosenthal, a very wise old couple living in the woods of Vermont. Don and Martha have committed their lives to exploring the ways of transformation through the medium of their relationship. After 50 years together, what began as a technique has now become a custom in their thriving relationship. It remains the simplest and most profound means of ensuring a lasting atmosphere for open-hearted communication.

There are always moments in your relationship when either you or your partner triggers a childhood Shadow reaction pattern, activating the Eden Loop. As you become more attentive and more aware of these moments, you will eventually be able to catch them as they occur. Sometimes you may be able to catch them before they occur. However, Don and Martha discovered that you could pre-empt and prevent these powerful triggering moments by changing the way you use language. Most emotional triggers occur because one person in the relationship uses a language and tone that activates a core unconscious belief that we are unworthy of being loved. Whether we react with anger, irritation, resentment, silence, guilt, or any other low frequency response, the source of our reaction in that moment is that we have forgotten to love and honour ourselves.

The first step in dismantling this pattern is to be aware of the trigger going off inside yourself. Despite this hurt you feel inside, you need to recognise that the pattern belongs to you, and even though the other person may have been insensitive, there is something important they are also trying to communicate to you. In such moments one of the hardest things to do is think of the other person's feelings as well as your own, but this is your challenge if you are to break the pattern of the Eden Loop. Usually at this point the urge you feel will be either to let the other know that they have hurt you, or you may turn away from them in some way. The words you choose to use in this moment are vital to breaking the pattern.

If you are to be able to discuss your feelings with another person without triggering their pattern, you can learn the art of 'joining'. Joining simply means that before you respond to what they said or did, you find a way to validate them. Validation is a technique commonly used in situations where emotions run high, and it can diffuse a great deal of misunderstanding. To validate someone you have to see life from their perspective. Below is an example of how to validate someone else's feelings:

Scenario 1 - Reacting

Partner 1: 'Why don't you ever do the dishes? I feel like it's always me that does them,'
Partner 2: 'I'm always doing them. I can't believe you say that. I bet if we kept a record, we'd see I have done them more often than you!'
The argument continues...

Scenario 2 - Joining

Partner 1: 'Why don't you ever do the dishes? I feel like it's always me that does them,'

Partner 2: 'You're right, I haven't done them for a while, and it must feel a bit like I'm not helping as much as usual. Here let me give you a hand.'

Although the above example may seem rather trite, it does demonstrate a universal truth – that most problems in communication are down to one or both partners not feeling that they are being listened to.

In the first scenario Partner 2 simply reacts in an unthinking and defensive way, which then triggers Partner 1's reaction pattern, and so the pattern repeats itself. It may well be that Partner 1's initial statement is based on their current feeling rather than a long term view, but it can easily be interpreted as an unjust judgement of Partner 2. However, for someone to say something like that, there must be some grain of truth to it, so it is probable that Partner 1 has not done the dishes at least in a short while!

In the 2nd Scenario we can see how joining works. Instead of instantly reacting on the assumption that Partner 1's statement is an indictment of their whole character, Partner 2 begins by empathising with Partner 1, validating their feelings. They also take a step towards Partner 1 by offering to help, instead of taking a step away. Not only is a conflict averted, but because Partner 1 feels supported and heard, they are now open to further communication. Partner 2 may have felt hurt or unjustly judged by the way Partner 1 expressed their initial cry for help, so if they need to they can share that, for example:

Partner 2: 'When you said you felt like you are always doing the dishes, it felt a bit unfair to me, as I often do them'.

Partner 1: 'Yes it must have seemed unfair, because you do do them quite a lot. I was just feeling a bit overwhelmed. I'm sorry about how it came out'.

Again, you can see here how Partner 1 has also validated Partner 2's feeling of injustice. This simple linking into the other person's inner state using language is how joining works. It ensures that a healthy open-hearted dialogue can continue. Initially when using a technique like this, it may feel a bit forced as you learn how to find the right words, but the more you practise this simple technique, the more subtle and natural it becomes. The power of the technique can be immediately seen when used in any situation where someone has been triggered into a deep emotional pattern.

THE PATHWAY OF INTELLIGENCE – A CASCADE OF CONSCIOUSNESS

As the Venus Stream continues to open us up to higher possibilities and frequencies, it can unlock an enormous creative intelligence within our relationship. This expanding energy field can be experienced like an emotional cascade. Its nature is to take us on a journey, and like a river, that journey sometimes goes through intense periods of transformation, which are usually followed by periods of calm. The Venus Stream will take us on an amazing ride, as we allow it to change the way we see ourselves and the way we relate with others.

Over time you will learn to respond to emotionally charged situations, while retaining your core stability and self love.

Every relationship offers us such a journey into higher consciousness, but our Dharma will continue to test us until we have burnt up all the Karma! It may take us the best part of a lifetime to allow ourselves to be transformed in this way. As in anything, we will go through periods of difficulty and periods of ease. Above all, this Pathway of Intelligence teaches us to let go of being defensive. This is why it offers us such a challenge, but it is the greatest challenge there is, and it comes with the greatest reward.

As we shall see, our reward is the breakthrough of unconditional love, as we pass through the subsequent Spheres of our EQ and our SQ.

8. THE SPHERE OF YOUR EQ

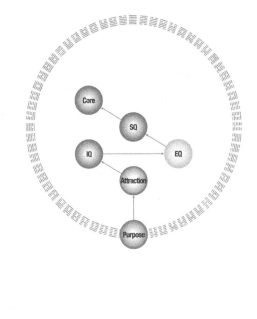

THE SPHERE OF YOUR EQ –
EMOTIONAL AWAKENING

The more deeply you explore the Gene Keys, the more you will realise how prophetic a transmission they are. They come at a time when humanity stands poised on the threshold of a great shift in consciousness. No matter where you look in the Gene Keys, you find evidence of this anticipation. The very structure and metaphor of the triple process of unfolding from Shadow to Gift to Siddhi is suggestive of our potential to move through this transition into a higher kind of life. The fuel that makes this transformation possible comes from the astral plane – from our emotions. When you read the 55th Gene Key, you will come to a section concerning the seven different 'Root Races' of humanity. This refers to the evolution of humanity as a whole, as we move through stages of collective frequency. Humanity has been transformed through different epochs – huge spans of time that allow for major evolutionary changes to occur. The next great consciousness shift, known as 'The Great Change' concerns the coming of the so-called 'Sixth Race':

The Sixth Race has long been prophesied by mystics and sages. Corresponding to the involution of Divine essence into the Astral Plane — the realm of emotion and desire — the Sixth Race will bring transformation to our entire planet. As Divine Consciousness continues to descend deeper and deeper into form, it reveals its true nature. The coming epoch will see the sublimation of human sexuality and desire into unconditional love. The Sixth Race will be triggered through the 55th Gene Key and its mutation within the solar plexus centre, the seat of human emotion. The Trivian Race heralds the reawakening of this centre and will allow human beings to experience once again the universal quantum field connecting all beings.

The 55th Gene Key

The Great Change spoken of in the 55th Gene Key refers to the time we are just now moving into, and it is being driven by a great emotional transformation within the genetic structure of human beings.

As we tread the Golden Path, we are journeying in microcosmic form into the heart of this revolution in consciousness, and the Venus Sequence describes the process through which the emotional charge latent in our relationships will trigger our next phase of collective awakening.

When we arrive at the Sphere of our EQ, we have come to the very apex of our emotional wound. Although the wound runs deeper than our emotions, it is here that the fire must burn the brightest in order that the transformation can take place. The human emotional journey is one of pleasure and pain, of passion and turmoil, of longing and despair, of ugliness and beauty. After we have made the transition through the Great Change, all this will have changed. We will be a different race of beings, less in the thrall of our emotional dramas, unburdened by the weight of our feelings. In essence we will no longer be victims of our emotions. It is in the Sphere of your EQ that you will find the core of your emotional challenges in this life. Here too you can turn your whole life around. You can lift yourself onto another plane of being.

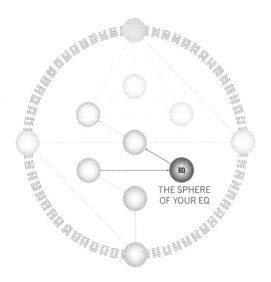

EQ: THE SECOND SEVEN YEARS (8-14)

EQ AND THE CYCLE OF PUBERTY

The Sphere of your EQ represents your emotional quotient – the measure of your emotional intelligence. It is relatively rare to find a human being who has a mature emotional intelligence.

Emotional intelligence has to do with three main things: our ability to listen, our ability to communicate clearly, and our willingness to take responsibility for our own feelings. The challenge of the Pathway of Intelligence is a juggling act between our IQ and our EQ, both of which are vital components of a well-rounded intelligence. Your EQ is imprinted during your 2nd 7-year cycle between the ages of 8 and 14. This phase of our childhood is the mid-ground between being a young child and becoming a young adult. Because this phase is in the middle of our childhood development, in many ways it is one of our greatest transitions in life.

From approximately the age of 11 or 12 most children enter into puberty. This is an intense period of chemical transition as new hormones are being released into the body. Our DNA is pre-coded to release these life-changing substances into our bloodstream as part of the awakening of our sexuality. During this phase of our young lives, it seems that everything about us is changing. As a parent you will watch your child at this stage accelerate away from their early innocence with a mixture of wonder, fascination, and perhaps a touch of sadness.

CROSSING THE RUBICON

One of the most well-rounded, sensitive, and holistic approaches to childhood education and development is the Steiner/Waldorf model. Conceived by the Austrian mystic Rudolf Steiner this approach considers the child from the deepest of angles. Steiner speaks of the three 7-year stages from birth to 21 as an ongoing process of incarnation in which the subtle bodies of the child are still literally coming into form. As in the Gene Keys view, the 2nd stage of development from 8 to 14 years also corresponds to the emotional development of the child. The beauty of the Steiner approach is that it has been tried and tested for over a century in thousands of schools around the globe.

Steiner teachers over the years have noted a powerful pattern occurring in children at around the age of nine years. This stage is known as 'crossing the Rubicon', which is a metaphor for a journey with no return. Corresponding with the loss of the child's milk teeth at around this age, the Rubicon represents the final transition from an experience of oneness with the world to the early development of the ego, or the sense of 'I'. Children at around this time begin to test their teachers' and parents' boundaries in a powerful new way. In another sense you could say that this is the child's final shaking off of the vestiges of Eden, as their consciousness begins to view the world from the perspective of a separate individual.

This extraordinary phase in our development is usually profoundly misunderstood by our parents and peers, who through no fault of their own are probably ignorant of what is really occurring. Were our teachers and parents aware of the momentous relevance of this time in our psychic and emotional development they would probably treat it very differently, with reverence and compassion, as opposed to discipline and harshness. Indeed most of modern education has no notion of the subtle development of the child. The adult view itself has little memory of life before the Rubicon. The Steiner approach has also noted another further transition connected to the Rubicon occurring at the later age of around eleven years. This is another period of transition in which children are seen to push hard against the edges of their conditioning. Steiner saw this as the beginnings of their fuller mental developmental stage, when the intellect first begins to lead the sense of 'I' within the child.

In such models of early development, it is wise not to be too prescriptive as some children develop early and others later. The 7-year cycles do not need to be interpreted literally but are intended as a broad guide. What you can see about this mid-phase of development is its huge relevance in the inner life of the child.

YOUR EQ IN RELATIONSHIPS – THE BOUNDARY ISSUE

One of the gauges of emotional maturity is a clear awareness of emotional boundaries. If your parents or peers did not imbue you with clear boundaries during your 2nd 7-year cycle, then this will emerge as a pattern later in life. Your EQ and its Gene Key and line may well give you further clues about potential boundary issues you experience in your relationships. The issue of boundaries is always a delicate balance. If you are too heavy-handed in dealing with a child in this phase, then they will rebel (either externally or internally) against being overly disciplined. No child wants to feel their wings clipped. Alternatively, if you do not apply firm enough boundaries but overindulge a child's needs and wishes, you will doubtless pay a price for this in their later teenage cycle of development. This 2nd phase of our development lays the groundwork for our equally challenging teenage cycle.

In later life we often fall to either side of a balanced sense of emotional boundaries. We may tend towards over-expressiveness of our emotions, which can lead to all kinds of confusion in our relationships. On the other hand we may be excessively guarded in our emotions, because of an excess of harshness we received as a child. Almost all emotional issues are rooted in this second phase of our childhood development, so it can be very revealing to go back in time and consider what kind of boundaries you experienced from your parents and teachers at this time.

Were your parents expressive of their own emotions? What were the quality and frequency of those emotions? Did they fight in front of you? Did they show love to each other and to you, and in what way?

It is important to overcome the tendency to want to blame our parents for our later emotional tendencies. They were doing the best they could with the tools they were given by their parents. The question is then: can we break the pattern of blame and resentment that may follow us into our own relationships? To do this we need to be well acquainted with our own patterns, and take full responsibility for them.

CHERISHING YOUR PRIMARY RELATIONSHIP – EMOTIONAL LOVE AFFAIRS

One of the common signs of a lack of boundaries in our primary relationship is the tendency to give our love inappropriately to people outside the relationship. Often we strike up a friendship (usually with a member of the opposite sex), where the feeling of love seems to flow more freely than in our own relationship. Dealing with this scenario with sensitivity is a hallmark of a healthy EQ. In our culture there is very little awareness of the whole concept of the emotional love affair. Perhaps we feel that we should be able to express love to others without our partner becoming jealous? Certainly this is true on one level, but the problems occur when we choose not to consider the feelings of our primary partner just because they may not be present. There is often general consensus that as long as we don't engage in any physical act of love, then everything else is allowed. This is clearly the mindset of a person who does not fully cherish their primary relationship.

Our primary relationship needs to be given centre stage in our life. If it is not, then it will inevitably wither. This is a universal truth. There is no point in being half-hearted when it comes to relationships. If you truly love someone, then you will love them enough to weather the storms that your karma throws up. If you enter into another relationship at an emotional level that in any way rivals your primary relationship, then trouble will follow sooner or later. It takes great maturity to love another person with appropriate boundaries and continue to honour your primary relationship. Honesty is paramount here. The simple rule to ask yourself is this: If my partner were here now, how would he or she feel about this? This consideration is part of the way you cherish your primary relationship. If this brings up issues of resentment inside you, then you must own those issues and dig deeper into their source.

Most of the time when we offer our love inappropriately to another outside of our primary relationship, it is because we are projecting that our partner is not meeting our needs in some way.

This is a golden opportunity if you use it wisely. It is not the role of your partner to meet all your emotional needs. This is precisely what the developing child learns in the 2nd cycle – that they have an independent emotional life that is no longer exclusively tied to their parent, and particularly to their mother. Emotional maturity means that you can express your emotional needs but without pressure or blame. It takes a real intelligence to be able to walk this line between expressing your inner emotional life, and simply realising that there are things that are better left unsaid.

CONTEMPLATION AND EMOTIONAL ALCHEMY

When you learn to cherish your partner and your relationship, then you will learn the art of leaving things unsaid. There are so many things that we feel are simply better transformed internally. There is a common misconception in our western culture that suggests that all emotions are best simply expressed in the moment they emerge. This is again an issue of boundaries. We have been told since the advent of Freud that emotions that are not expressed can be damaging to us. To an extent it is true that the repression of emotions and desires is indeed a dangerous thing. The more we try and battle a feeling, the more power we give it.

There is however another path – the path of emotional alchemy. Many feelings can be allowed, accepted, and embraced internally. They can be shared if appropriate, but a great deal of our emotional life (particularly our emotional Shadows) is best transformed internally. Again, another sign of a healthy EQ is enough consideration for others not to lay all of our emotional issues at their feet. We each have enough to deal with just with our own issues!

HOW THEN DO WE ACHIEVE THIS INTERNAL ALCHEMY?

When we train the lens of contemplation on the sphere of our EQ, it naturally transforms into a deeper kind of emotional awareness. Emotional contemplation involves being with our feelings in a new and powerful way.

We make the commitment to draw our intense feelings inward without in any way repressing them. In a nutshell we allow them time inside us. So many arguments and conflicts erupt in relationships, because we indulge our feelings in the moment that they occur. This is a challenging habit to break! Emotional contemplation can help us break this habit by simply retaining the feelings, impulses, and words in a holding bay inside us. If we give them a little more time, many emotions simply dissolve or transform all on their own.

'KEEPING IT IN THE PORCH' – AN EMOTIONAL COMMITMENT WHILE TRAVELLING THE GOLDEN PATH

In the UK, many houses have a small external room or covering built over the front door. Known as the porch, this serves as a transitionary area where coats and boots are often taken off and hung up before we enter into the house fully. As you learn the art of emotional contemplation, you can make an inner commitment to yourself regarding this new way of handling your emotions in relationships. This is the 2nd major technique of the Venus Sequence. We learn to 'keep our emotions in the porch'. Instead of simply allowing the stream of our emotions to come pouring out without any awareness, we give them a moment of pause.

Keeping our feelings in the porch does not mean that we hold back from expressing ourselves. It simply means that we acknowledge that some things are better unsaid and we need time to see what, if anything, does need to be said. If we have held our feelings in the metaphorical porch for a while and they still want to come out, then that is also okay. But the chances are they will emerge in a different, more considered and diplomatic way.

This technique of simply holding onto our low frequency emotions for a while, instead of blurting them out is so simple that most people have never considered it! It is however the basis of emotional alchemy. You may have realised by now that contemplation demands a slow and easy rhythm, and this is particularly the case when we are dealing with emotions. Emotions are dynamic - and as their name suggests – they are energy in motion. If you hold back some of that pressure, it can move through a transformation onto a higher plane.

THE UPSIDE OF YOUR EQ - DEFENCE OR DANCE

As you employ these simple techniques and insights, you will soon see what a hub of transformation the Sphere of your EQ really is. It is the first place where the sacred wound emerges onto the emotional/astral plane. This means that there is an enormous charge in this Sphere. As you bring deeper awareness into the patterns of this Gene Key in your life, you will find that two things happen – the first is that you will begin to drop your defences in relationships. Dropping your defences is not the same as dropping your boundaries. Whenever we feel emotionally threatened, we contract into a defensive pattern that we learned in our childhood. By slowing down the intensity of our emotional life, we take the sting out of this pattern. The second thing that occurs as we transform these emotional shadow patterns internally is that we feel a new buoyancy inside. Figuratively speaking, we begin to want to dance.

The upside of our EQ is that we rekindle a lost part of our childhood – our love of play. The very energy that goes into defending ourselves from the perceived threats of others is released into our life as a spirit of playfulness. When the Gene Key of your EQ is positively released at a higher frequency, this quality emerges in a very playful manner. All the joys of our childhood remain inside our DNA throughout our lives as stored potential delight. If our childhood wounding patterns can persist into adulthood, it makes sense that our childhood wonders can also persist. This is the reward of achieving a balanced EQ. We no longer need to look outside ourselves to have our emotional needs met, because our joyousness keeps welling up from within. From this place we are able for the first time in a long, long time to live in a relationship in a truly healthy way.

THE SHADOW

The Shadow and line of the Gene Key in the Sphere of your EQ will consistently undermine your Core Stability. This is an emotional pattern, so even if the Gene Key you have here has a strong mental bias, it will be in conjunction with your emotional makeup. A lack of emotional intelligence often manifests as a tendency to get caught up in blaming others. We blame others for our condition, because we are unable or unwilling to take full responsibility for it. In most cases we are not even aware of our emotional Shadow patterns, but have simply become accustomed to indulging in them.

The Shadow of your EQ often has to do with the indulgence of the low frequency state. It is a sad fact that we often save our worst behaviour for those we claim to love the most. As we have seen, an important aspect of having a high EQ is consideration for those we love. Instead of indulging in our negativity just because we can, we either sublimate it into something creative, or we draw it inside and allow it to be transformed. Look deeply into the Shadow of your EQ, and you will find its roots going back to your 2nd childhood cycle. Then move into a deep contemplative process with this pattern until you have seen how and when it emerges in your life. Under what conditions do you forget to be kind to those you love? Once you have got to the bottom of this pattern, you will find it much easier to transform.

THE GIFT

The Gifts of your EQ are manifold and wonderful. This is about bringing the best of your childhood alive again. We all need to play in life. Life can be hard and serious at times, but it can also be filled with wonder and delight. As you learn to transcend and transform the victim patterns of the Shadow of your EQ, you will give birth to the eternal spirit of the inner child once again. Look into the Gift of the Gene Key of your EQ, and consider how much joy and fun you could spread through a full expression of this Gift and its line. There are places within our psyche where we are simply never supposed to grow up. On contemplating this Gift you might like to consider the dreams and gifts you had as a child passing through this mid cycle of your childhood. What are your happiest, most golden memories of that time? You can breathe in the essence of those memories, and then find a way to integrate them once again in your current life. We have already seen the hallmarks of a healthy EQ – a strong sense of emotional accountability, the ability to consider the feelings of others at all times, the dropping of our defensiveness, and the ability to retain clear emotional boundaries. All of these are the qualities of a mature emotional adult. However, the final flowering of your EQ is always about revelling in your innocence, in the simple joys of life and in your ability to think, act, and play like a child once again.

THE SIDDHI

The Siddhi of your EQ concerns the transmutation of low frequency emotional charge into a higher form of creativity.

The clearer you become in your relationships, the more you cherish them and the more devotional energy you will feel. Relationships and friendships are the true wonder of human life. Each relationship is an odyssey that offers us an opportunity for deep transformation. At their highest, your relationships can become the most direct path available in the modern world to an awareness of your inherent Divinity. The Siddhis represent the bringing in of our inner harvest. This usually comes after much inner work and through having undergone many trials. We all at some point move through a deep process of grieving over our relationships - either through a relationship that comes to an end or the death of a loved one.

The Siddhi of your EQ is a constant reminder of the ray of light that always lies behind the emotional process of relating. At their highest frequencies your emotions can be such beautiful, poetic reachings into the void. Emotion itself has to be burned up before we can move into those states of inner silence and transcendence. Therefore as we come closer to such states, our emotions become so sweet and exquisite that they make our hearts ache for the beyond.

Such states of devotion and bhakti always precede the final flowering of our hearts. Ponder deeply on the Siddhi of your EQ for it holds the key to your emotional transcendence.

THE 6 LINES OF YOUR EQ

The 6 lines of your EQ are a view into your basic ideology. In the Venus Sequence we distinguish the words Psychology and Ideology by attaching them to the two different realms of the IQ and the EQ respectively. Thus your ideology refers to a core emotional attitude that you evolve primarily through your 2nd 7-year cycle. Because it is during this phase that you develop your full independent ego, it is also when you get your first real taste of what it means to relate to another as separate from yourself. Your ideology therefore runs very deeply inside you. It informs and motivates your psychology, the mental attitudes you evolve more fully in your 3rd cycle of development.

THE SPHERE OF YOUR EQ

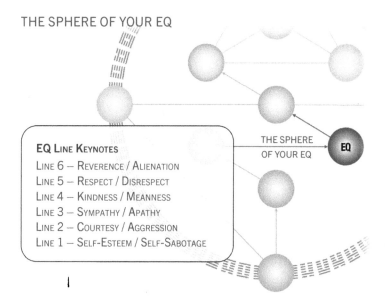

EQ LINE KEYNOTES

LINE 6 — REVERENCE / ALIENATION
LINE 5 — RESPECT / DISRESPECT
LINE 4 — KINDNESS / MEANNESS
LINE 3 — SYMPATHY / APATHY
LINE 2 — COURTESY / AGGRESSION
LINE 1 — SELF-ESTEEM / SELF-SABOTAGE

THE SPHERE
OF YOUR EQ

EQ

EQ KEYNOTES (IDEOLOGY)

Line 1: Self-Esteem / Self-sabotage

You can see from this 1st line that the whole foundation stone of our emotional wound is the issue of self-esteem. Depending on the patterns that developed in our first seven-year cycle, some of us will carry deeper issues of self-esteem than others. The focus of the 1st line is always inwards, so at a low frequency this is a self-undermining pattern. Because of the universal nature of the sacred wound we all carry issues of self-esteem, and they tend to come up during times of emotional conflict. It is important to look at the repressive and reactive tendencies of the Gene Key of your EQ, so that you can see the full spectrum of ways in which you might undermine yourself if you have a 1st line EQ.

This is a pattern where you may stubbornly insist on a course of action that you know will only lead to more suffering, but you seem unable to prevent yourself. Of course, once you begin to see that this behaviour emerged as a form of emotional defence when you were young, you should find it easier to dismantle the pattern as an adult.

Sometimes self-sabotage can be very subtle. Our physical body will often betray a deeper emotional symptom that we are not admitting to ourselves. Honest contemplation of your deepest feelings will always reveal the truth of how you really feel inside yourself. Sometimes we simply need to shine more of the razor-like light of awareness deeper into our emotional lives than we might feel comfortable with. On the other hand, once you are aware of your tendency to sabotage your own and other's joyousness, the deep foolishness of such a stance can be a powerful leveller. You may well find that you have healed a deep and lasting emotional pattern with relative ease. The healthy 1st line will always have a strong sense of self-esteem coupled with a good dose of humility. Self-esteem is such a beautiful and influential trait, and if you have a 1st line EQ, you can constantly remind yourself that it is your natural inner emotional state.

Line 2: Courtesy / Aggression

By its nature the 2nd line does not tend to easily keep things inside. Feelings have a habit of just popping out very readily! This can either be a great gift when it is appropriately channeled, or it can be very detrimental, both to yourself and to others. In relationships, the 2nd line's most common low frequency expression is aggressiveness. The 2nd line is a natural conduit for powerful emotions such as anger, and anger with blame attached becomes aggression. As a child this was the pattern you may have learned that seemed to make you feel more in control of your emotional environment – to attack as a form of defence. Aggression can take many forms, some subtler and more passive than others.

The subtlest form of aggression can come simply through the tone of your voice. Because of the passion of the 2nd line, it can be very challenging to overcome such a deeply ingrained pattern.

The high frequency of the 2nd line EQ is courtesy. We have already seen the importance of this quality in all relationships, and the 2nd line is the champion of courtesy. Courtesy is not perhaps as it might sound – it is not all restrained delicacy and politeness. It is passion directed with consideration. Powerful emotions like anger can be released without blame. The anger can simply be released in a pure manner, or it can be channeled through some creative medium. The 2nd line nature is all about free self-expression, and without awareness this can be very destructive to the peace of any relationship. With awareness and courtesy, self-expression can take place in a non-reactive way. In fact, free self-expression with awareness can be hugely powerful as a way of re-affirming your own and other's self-esteem. This is the true power of the 2nd line - to make others feel good about themselves.

Line 3: Sympathy / Apathy

The healthy 3rd line EQ is the kind of person you will always want to turn to when you are experiencing difficulty or pain. Such people have a way of making you feel instantly comfortable, accepted, and emotionally at ease. The same pattern at a low frequency however will always invite suspicion.

These may be interesting people, but there will always be something about them that sets you ill at ease. This is a pattern of emotional apathy. Apathy means that at some deep level you have suppressed the emotions that make you feel vulnerable. This pattern will have first been imprinted between the ages of 8 and 14, when we experienced emotional pressure either from our peer group, or when we turned away from our parents in some way. Apathy involves shutting yourself off from intense feelings, which in turn makes you less able to sense or be aware of the feelings of others. If you have a 3rd line EQ, then you need to carefully consider and contemplate the ways you try and deflect intense emotions.

Sometimes the 3rd line EQ can make a good pretence of being emotional, but the reality is that often the emotions only exist on the surface. Emotional awareness is about moving through your own process and coming out the other side, whereas the 3rd line can find ways of never resolving an issue but remain in a kind of eternal emotional loop. The secret for the 3rd line is to break out of their pattern of self-obsession. The 3rd line has a natural gift for understanding the full emotional spectrum from sadness to joy. This is what makes them masters of sympathy – because they can be vulnerable without being over-indulgent. You have to be vulnerable in order to resonate in true sympathy with another person, because you can allow your own emotions to respond to theirs without losing your own sense of self in the process. You can consider this in the light of your Gift and Siddhi in the Sphere of your EQ.

Line 4: Kindness / Meanness

The 4th line is a classic pattern that we all learn as we move through our childhood. Particularly as we begin to relate with the opposite sex this pattern comes to the fore. Meanness is an externalisation of our own low self-esteem. It is also a way of pushing someone else away when we fear rejection by them. The 4th line has a natural social gift, so as these children develop through puberty they can use this gift to manipulate others in their social circle.

Although meanness can be direct at times, most of the time it is an indirect pattern, used behind another person's back for example. The 4th line can be very political in this way. If you have a 4th line EQ, then you need to look honestly at your behaviour when you feel rejected by another. How do you reject others? Do you use subtle tactics, and are you aware of such tactics?

Meanness is simply the other side of kindness. Kindness is the natural expression of the 4th line as it flows out of your self-esteem. If you feel good about yourself, then you will always wish to share this feeling with others. The 4th line can be very saintly in this way, giving of itself without expectation of return.

True kindness is also often hidden. Out of consideration for another person's feelings, you might choose not to say something that you know would hurt them. Such small acts of kindness usually go unseen, but at the same time they help propagate harmony. If you have a 4th line EQ, consider the Gift and the Siddhi of the Gene Key of this Sphere as a quality you can offer to others in all your relationships. Meanness makes us feel bad, whereas kindness always makes us feel good. It may be obvious, but it also tells us something profound about life – that it truly pays to be kind.

Line 5: Respect / Disrespect

The final two lines of the Sphere of EQ are Respect and Reverence, which both bring the whole subject of emotional wounding and transformation to a climax. The 5th line as we have seen repeatedly throughout the Golden Path always carries this potential for respect. This is what imbues the 5th line with its special quality as a leader. And it is here that the respect emerges – from an emotional maturity that can immediately be sensed by others. At the Shadow frequency however, the 5th line falls into the trap of disrespect.

Disrespect can manifest in so many different forms – it can be a lack of respect for one's body, one's own health, or for feelings in general. Or disrespect can be projected outwards onto the environment, the culture, or specific people. Disrespect is an energy field that can also be subtle – it can come over as impatience, cynicism, ingratitude, or selfishness. Sometimes the 5th line will abuse its powers of leadership and influence by pursuing their own agenda and ignoring the wider impact they have on the world. We see this pattern in many influential people in the modern world. It is interesting then that this will to increase one's power is linked to a deep-seated emotional insecurity.

If you have a 5th line EQ, then your emotional Shadow issues are always about power struggles, so you might like to consider the deeper worldview that lies beneath these patterns. Many successful people are damaged emotionally.

Emotional transformation for the 5th line therefore often involves a process of deep humbling, in which there is often some kind of a fall from grace. It usually takes a powerful event to shake the 5th line awake from its deep need to try and increase its sense of power. An emotionally healthy EQ always carries this humility into the world, and it is this sense of internal radiant power and confidence coupled with humility that draws the respect of others.

The key to gaining respect from others is of course to respect oneself first and foremost, and this precludes that you are really familiar with your own Shadows.

Line 6: Reverence / Alienation

When we come to the 6th line, we move from Respect to Reverence. Although these two themes are connected, they manifest as very different gifts in the world. Although it is founded upon respect for all creatures, reverence is not in any way about issues of power. The 6th line is not designed to be a

139

leader like the 5th line. The 6th line does not carry that radiant magnetic quality of the 5th line. More than any of the lines, the 6th line is a journey whose themes change throughout your life. If you have a 6th line EQ, then your life will be a voyage of emotional discovery. It may not be an easy journey since the final goal of the journey is emotional wisdom, and that can only be attained after many trials. Having said this, the 6th line has an amazing staying power, and this inner resilience is held up by a deep vision. The danger is that at the Shadow frequencies, we lose touch with the vision. The vision will always be some kind of unconscious knowing that one day we will find out what true love really feels like.

The 6th line has to be the most patient of all the lines. Emotions are the new arena of human transformation, and people with a 6th line EQ are the pioneers of a new understanding of the emotional plane. The Shadow keynote of the 6th line EQ is Alienation. Every 6th line will inherently know what this means, and will feel it as a theme that comes and goes throughout their lives. Reverence is about honouring the long-term view. It is about experiencing the full spectrum of emotions and above all, being compassionate towards oneself.

Sometimes the 6th line may feel as though it's travelling through a tunnel, and at certain times you emerge and are flooded by the light. Then you move into another phase where you are once again in the tunnel. This whole process has a purpose. It cannot be controlled, but must be surrendered to and embraced. In the end, you will become stronger, more open-hearted, and more conscious of the beauty of life than you can ever imagine. This is the true meaning of reverence.

CONTEMPLATING YOUR EQ

As you can see, the Sphere of your EQ is something of a plunge into your watery depths. For most of us, this inner emotional healing is a labour of love that we will engage in for most of our lives. It is the place where our wounding is at its most tender, before it has reached the mind, but not as deep as our physical structure, where it emerges from. As you learn what it means to contemplate your life at an emotional level, you will increase the pitch of your emotional life. Feelings may well become more intense as the light of awareness shines upon them. Hidden feelings may also emerge, as you plumb the depths of the ideology that was formed out of the emotional challenges you experienced when you were young.

The allegory of your EQ is reflected in the image of a river that moves over rapids, cascades and even at times, waterfalls. This part of your Venus Sequence will take you on an emotional journey that at times seems turbulent and out of control, and at other times seems calm and at peace. The Venus Stream unlocks our sequence inside us in this way.

Emotional patterns contain powerful charges held within the DNA, and as your awareness unlocks each pattern you can either be overwhelmed by it and go under, or you can steer yourself down the cascade into safer and quieter waters. The other aspect of this work is that it will test you over and over again. Sometimes you will succeed and keep your head above the water, and sometimes you will forget and take the plunge.

It is important to be patient and compassionate with yourself. It takes time to bring awareness into such deep-seated patterns and Shadows.

Above all, contemplation on your EQ will enhance your relationships. This is like polishing the mirror of your relationships so that nothing can remain hidden from you. You must remember two things above all: the first is to be accountable for your own feelings. They emerge from within your own DNA and although they may be triggered by others, it is up to you to learn how to handle them inside yourself in a way that is respectful to you and others. The second thing of paramount importance is always to keep a wider perspective on your life. It is easy for us to become bogged down in our Shadow patterns, expecting them to change or be transformed overnight. Our Shadows are a part of who we are, and this work is about integrating all aspects of our nature, both the wonderful parts and the unpleasant bits!

The Venus Sequence is an intense spiritual and emotional work to undertake, and it requires commitment. But it also doesn't have to all be heavy and hard work all the time. We all need to keep taking those pauses where we simply switch off, go out into nature, take a holiday, have a drink, watch a film, and do whatever brings us joy. You are a human being of many ages, and you carry the wound of ages. But you also carry the light of divinity inside your DNA, and this will continue to shine even when you may have forgotten it.

We are a house of many mansions, a spectrum of different wavelengths and moods. We are an easel for consciousness to explore itself upon. You may not even understand the depths of the work you are undertaking as you travel this Golden Path.

You may wonder whether anything is happening at all. These are natural states and feelings, and are a part of the greater journey itself. The secret of this work is simply to keep carrying on.

If you get lost, you can always come back to that place of trust. It always exists inside you. So free yourself from the idea that your journey must be a certain way. It is exactly as it is supposed to be in every moment. In the words of the ancient Sufis:

Al Safar Zafar! Voyaging is Victory!

9. THE PATHWAY OF LOVE

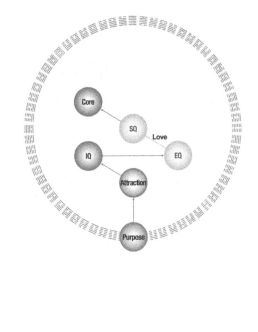

DISCOVERING THE ESSENTIAL IN YOUR LIFE

It has been said by many wise people that there are two paths to God. One is the Path of Meditation, and the other is the Path of Love. The Path of Meditation leads men and women away from the world into the retreats of inner silence and lonely contemplation. This path is well documented in all traditions and there exists an abundance of structured paths and teachings to follow, from Buddhism to Sufism to Christianity. The Path of Love however leads us not away from society and culture but right into its beating heart. The Path of Love is the path of human relationship, of service and devotion. Because of its nature the Path of Love is a wilder path. It emerges as we interact with life and the people and circumstances of our Dharma. It is a beautiful paradox that both paths lead to the same place – the Path of Meditation leads to love and the Path of Love leads to meditation.

In the Venus Sequence, we follow the Path of Love. We use our daily lives and our relationships as the fuel of our spiritual transformation. This means that if you have a primary relationship, then you must place that relationship at the heart of your life. If you do not happen to have a primary relationship at the moment, then you must place all relationships at the heart of your life. If you are not able to make either of these inner commitments, it is better to be honest with yourself, and you may find that your natural path is that of meditation. If there is something that is more important to you than your loved one – your personal goals, your work or career for example, then you need to re-examine your commitment to the Path of Love. The Venus Sequence is a coded pathway that lies within every human being. It is a clear path towards spiritual realisation and eventual transcendence, but like all such undertakings, it requires a strong inner commitment.

Whatever your feelings are in response to the above, they are perfectly acceptable. The realisation of what is essential in life is a process. The only essential is love, but for many of us this realisation must come of its own accord and in its own timing.

If however you have already realised this Truth – that the only essential is love – then you are truly ready to begin this work with your Venus Sequence. The great advantage of the Path of Love is that it is completely inclusive. You can pursue your personal goals in life, and still be right on the Path of Love. Indeed, the Venus Sequence requires that you follow your outer purpose in life. The only question here is one of priorities; the following question is therefore a litmus test of your commitment:

Are you willing to prioritise your primary relationship above all other aspects of your life?

And if you happen to be single:

Are you willing to prioritise relationships above all other aspects of your life?

You will notice that the questions above do not speak overtly of prioritising love. This is because sometimes our relationships do not always feel loving. Sometimes a relationship with a parent, a partner, or a child can seem incredibly challenging. Your commitment must be to the relationship in all its seasons, with all its karma. Nothing less than a total commitment will serve to unlock the fullness of your Venus Sequence. A 99% commitment in this is no different from a 1% commitment.

In the Venus Sequence, the Pathway of Love is a powerful contemplation of the level of importance you give to love in your everyday life. Like each of the Pathways along the Golden Path, this is an exciting journey rather than a static measurement. The Pathway of Love links the Sphere of your EQ to the Sphere of your SQ, and as you will see, your SQ describes you living your life with a permanently open heart. It is the source of all love. What this means is that as you travel the meandering pathways of your Venus Sequence, you are called upon to surrender more and more of your ego in the name of love. Through the Sphere of your IQ, you must move beyond your mind and its tendency to undermine you. In the Sphere of your EQ, you must let go of the emotional patterns you have learned that keep closing your heart off to others.

When your awareness awakens fully in the Sphere of your SQ, you will return to a simpler more loving state that lies beyond the cries of the mind and the needs and urges of the emotions. It is here in this Pathway of Love that we learn once and for all to drop our ego and embrace a higher calling – the only essential there is – the call of Love.

THE BREAKTHROUGH AND THE FLOOD

Our major work with the Venus Sequence takes place in the Spheres of the IQ and the EQ. We have already likened the Pathway of Intelligence that links these Spheres to the first Pathway of Challenge in the Activation Sequence. It follows then that the Pathway of Love is also a Pathway of Breakthrough, and this is most certainly the case. In the Venus Sequence, the breakthrough is about love. As we begin to learn to transcend the ebb and flow of our emotions, we experience a profound opening of the heart. Unlike the emotional journey, it doesn't come in fits and starts, but comes all at once as a flood. We are flooded by the love that is released from within our DNA.

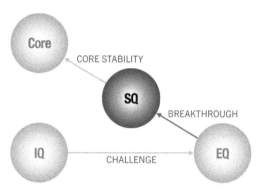

THE SQ - EMOTIONAL BREAKTHROUGH

The flood of love can only come when the dam inside us bursts. This can be a very intense aspect of working with your Venus Sequence, because it involves getting in touch with the sacred wound inside your body.

There will be times when you feel overwhelmed by a profound feeling of Isolation. Isolation is the Shadow keynote of this Pathway of Love. This sense of Isolation can come in many ways – it can come as depression, anxiety, rage, grief, melancholy, or any other intensely uncomfortable feeling. Such feelings seem to go beyond the normal emotional spectrum. They seem to be lodged so deeply inside us that we feel they may never leave. You need to be alert to periods in which you find yourself in such a state, because despite what you may feel, you are touching the edge of holiness.

The sacred wound lives inside each of us. It manifests as a vast sense of Isolation, in which we cannot feel our heart, in which we appear to be rendered powerless. Often the wound is a physical sensation localised in the body. If you tune into your body, you may be able to sense where the wound appears for you. Sometimes the wound is not local, but a general numbing of all our faculties. Such states often precede the breakthrough of great love, but we must stay with the wound, wrapping our awareness around it for as long as it takes for the transformation to occur. This is how our great love has been dammed, and when the dam bursts, we experience a state of grace – a euphoric expansion throughout our body, and in particular our chest, as the flood of love breaks through.

SUPPORT IN MELTING THE ISOLATION

When we work with our heart as we journey through the Venus Sequence, there are times when it is appropriate to have outside support. Particularly as we get in touch with the cosmic wound inside us, a part of our healing may be to allow another to witness us in that vulnerable state and offer us solace and support. If we are looking for support, it is vital however to find someone who can truly empathise with you in that state. If you know such a person, then they will probably spring to mind right away. It is important to know that you are not looking to find someone who can help you get out of the uncomfortable state you may be in.

We do not need to be fixed. We need to feel loved and accepted. Often the best form of support comes through physical touch, since it bypasses both mind and emotions and goes straight into the physical structure itself. In this respect, a really good intuitive bodyworker can help you to accept and embrace the more difficult moments of your transformation.

THE TENDERNESS OF THE UNIVERSAL MOTHER

As your awareness probes more deeply back into the patterns of your past, it will begin to explore the states of consciousness you inhabited in the first 7 years of your life. This period is mythically dominated by a single over-arching figure – your mother. Regardless of your personal circumstances, your first 7-year cycle depicts the story of your relationship to a mother figure, whoever that is. Obviously in most cases this is your mother herself, although it can also be the father or indeed any other person. While in the womb we are held in the universal spirit of tenderness, and it is rare that a mother does not feel this same spirit of unconditional love towards their child at birth. Only the most intense personal trauma can dull such a special form of love.

Whenever we get in touch with the sacred wound inside, we unconsciously cry out for this same spirit of tenderness represented by the mother. When you journey into the Sphere of your SQ, you will discover that this universal spirit actually exists everywhere at all times, and is not dependent on any other human being. This is the crux of our inner healing. All of our relationship issues and struggles can be traced back to this deep internal cry for the tender touch of the universal Mother. As you begin to lift free from the emotional ties and Shadows of your EQ, so you will be following in the footsteps of those great souls who have walked the Pathway of Love before you. Reading and imbibing the words of these ecstatics can be a further bolster to your heart, as you continue in your epic voyage along the Golden Path.

10. THE SPHERE OF YOUR SQ

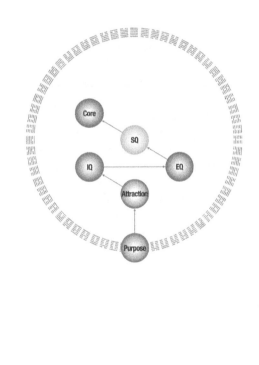

THE SPHERE OF YOUR SQ – OPENING YOUR HEART THROUGH RELATIONSHIPS

When we get to the Sphere of SQ, then we have really arrived at the hub of our healing journey. Your SQ is your spiritual quotient – the measure of your ability to remain connected to the spiritual heart of life. The Venus Sequence is keynoted as a process that is all about opening your heart through relationships. It's interesting to consider how this flows outwards into your 4 Prime Gifts, which are to do with discovering your genius. The expression of your genius is rooted in the opening of your heart, and the breakthrough of your Radiance is a mirror of this deeper breakthrough of the unconditional love that comes from your SQ. This is why your Profile is 'hologenetic', because like a hologram these breakthroughs ripple out into your life simultaneously at different levels within your psyche. An increase in awareness at any level has a holographic ripple effect that travels throughout your entire being.

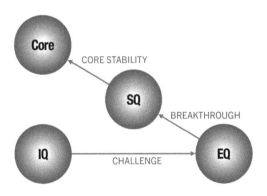

SQ: EMOTIONAL BREAKTHROUGH

We have also seen that our IQ governs our psychology and our EQ our ideology. Your SQ governs your mythology – the unconscious contours of the longing of your soul to return home.

The SQ is centred on the myth of homecoming, because it has always been the heart that is our true home. As long as you feel love, then you are home. This is the origin of the word 'hearth' – the home fire that always burns in the centre of your house. The flood of love that comes through the Pathway of Love comes from your SQ, which is like the grail that constantly gives forth of itself. The Sphere of your SQ is also the only Sphere that doesn't have a Shadow keynote, because it is the only place inside that is truly innocent. As you enter into contemplation of your SQ, you can look at its Gene Key and line in this way. Although you may have learned the ways of its Shadow, it was something that was put into you when you were too young to do anything about it, so the journey into your SQ is a journey of retrieval and recovery. This is the eternal flame of unconditional love inside you, and all you have to do is keep asking for it back.

THE FIRST SEVEN YEARS

One of the most poignant questions that often comes from parents involved in the Golden Path process is: how can I best help my children as they develop through these various 7-year cycles? The simple answer to this question is by increasing your awareness of your own Shadow patterns. The sacred wound is an integral part of life's journey, and everyone carries it in their DNA before they are even born. The final Pathway of the Venus Sequence, the Pathway of Realisation, represents the way in which the sacred wound is imprinted right into our physiological structure as we are growing in the womb. Although the mother can subtly influence the foetus through maintaining a calm inner state as much as possible, nevertheless, the wound will still one day emerge.

Once the child is born, our dharma begins to unravel. The events of the outer world begin to impact us – the inner state of our parents, brothers and sisters, the culture we inhabit, the physical environment and its sounds, smells, and tastes – everything combines to shape our destiny. Other than the nine months of gestation, no cycle has a greater impact on our future than the first seven years of our lives.

As adults we tend to see young children through adult eyes, since most of us have long forgotten that time before the Rubicon. These first seven years really represent a kind of Eden consciousness, in which we do not experience ourselves as fully separate from our surroundings. We live in a natural state of wonder, and we will spend most of our lives unconsciously trying to return.

Adults who are committed to the process of opening the heart are relatively rare. Many of us attempt this momentous task, but many of us are unable to do the deep transformation necessary. This is where the power of staying in a relationship can pay off. Most divorces occur in a child's first seven years when the pressure on the parents is greatest. It takes a profound selflessness to devote one's life to the bringing up of a child. Whether you are a parent or not, you were once a child and you also took this difficult journey where you experienced what it feels like to leave the Garden of Eden. Your SQ, your spiritual quotient, is a measure of how deeply you allow yourself to feel this sense of separation and the wholeness that lies behind it.

The long answer to the question of how best to support young children is to take the journey of transformation back to your own lost youth. We must learn once again to see through our hearts, with the sense of utter trust that comes when we are very young. As Christ said: '...except ye turn, and become as little children, ye shall in no wise enter into the kingdom of heaven'. And the place where we must learn that level of trust is in our relationships.

YOUR SQ — LIVING A MYTHIC LIFE

We have passed through our IQ and the formation of our psychology, the EQ and the formation of our ideology, now we come to the SQ, which represents our life mythology. What does it mean to live a mythic life, and how do we go about it? Joseph Campbell, the great mythologist summarised his life's work through the immortal line: 'follow your bliss'. It takes a leap of courage to follow your bliss. It is not the same as following your pleasure. Bliss is rooted in a deep transcendence of your suffering, so to follow your bliss is to move deeper into the nature of your suffering. Your SQ calls you to a great life. It will transform the mundane into the mystical, it will allow you to live as a hero or heroine in the drama of your life.

In many people weighed down by the culture, conditioning, and distractions of the modern age, the SQ is simply asleep. The flood of unconditional love never passes along the Pathway of Love, because it is kept in check by the Shadow patterns of the EQ and the IQ. As Thoreau said: 'most men lead lives of quiet desperation'. To embark upon a mythical life is to step towards your fear rather than hide from it. If you are reading this and have come this far in the Golden Path Program, there must be a fire burning strongly inside you. The Gene Keys are not an easy quick-fix system that tell you what to do. They are a deep mythic tapestry of insight, and the Golden Path puts the full responsibility of awakening back onto you where it belongs.

When you contemplate your SQ, and the Gene Key and line of your SQ, spend some serious time with it. Every Gene Key has a mythological association. Look into the archetypes that haunt your higher consciousness. Which heroes and heroines are you most drawn to? Which Gods and Goddesses? Which cultures? Your psyche is littered with clues. Look objectively at your bookshelves. Recall the fairy tales and fables that most strongly impacted you as a young child. Dig deeply into your being for your mythology, and see how it is reflected by the Gene Key of your SQ. Your SQ is like the deep ocean before the flood. It is the place you must dive into to find the pearls and sunken treasure of your long lost childhood. Dig and you will find it. Contemplate for long enough and a face will emerge from beneath those waves.

INCARNATION - THE IMPRINTING OF THE PHYSICAL BODY

In the New Age many people speak of the process of reincarnation – the notion of a separate soul that enters into different bodies and experiences a succession of lifetimes.

Perhaps not so much consideration is given simply to the process of incarnation itself. To 'in-carnate' literally means to come into the form or 'meat', and it is not simply about being born. Birth is the second beginning after conception. According to the Gene Keys revelation, it takes 21 years (3 X 7 year cycles) to incarnate fully. Even then, most people never complete the process to its fullest extent, but get caught by the Shadow frequencies, with certain fundamental aspects still hovering outside of the form. The Golden Path is in effect a process of re-incarnation as we revisit our first 21 years and rewire our behaviour patterns, bringing our full higher being down into the form of our physical bodies.

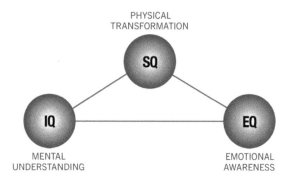

IQ, EQ AND SQ - TRINITY OF TRANSFORMATION

It is in the first 7 years of our lives that our physical body learns to live in the world. Even though we may develop a rudimentary emotional awareness and our brain development begins, the real focus of our lives is exploring the physical plane through our physiology, our senses, and our sense of will. Young children quickly manifest a strong will in their early years, as they learn to push up against the boundaries of physical reality. In their early years children literally swim in the frequencies of life. Being fresh from the void, they are still half in the dream of non-existence and half in their new dream of existence. As adults we usually do not realise how sensitive a young child really is.

They feel so keenly every frequency you emit, and they take it in at such a physical and visceral level that it actually becomes woven into the form of their physical structure. As the child's organs develop, they are programmed by the quantum environment in which the child lives. This is why it is so important to be aware when you are with young children. Not only does your attitude affect them, it is built into them.

In the light of the above, you might like to consider the atmosphere - physical, emotional, and mental - that you were brought up in. There is no cause for alarm as you contemplate such things. It is good to be aware of the programming environment that you grew up in. Knowing the prevalent patterns of your parents can greatly help you to see why you carry certain wounds into your later relationships. You should also consider the higher frequencies of your parents and caregivers, and how those frequencies were also imprinted into your physical DNA as you grew. Even though you carry your own unique higher purpose, you are also a blend of the frequencies that surrounded you as a child.

One of the greatest head-starts for a young child is to be in a natural environment – to be able to run and stumble through the grasses and trees, and to learn from and be absorbed in the elements – water, earth, air, and fire. Young children also have a natural affinity with animals, birds, insects, and all manner of creatures. An upbringing among such things is a great blessing for a child, and if they receive the frequencies of nature consistently in their first 7 years, they will develop a naturally strong and healthy constitution. Most important of all however is of course love. The young child knows love as a fish knows water. It is their home. A lack of love is like a lack of air for any young child, and there is no love like the love of a parent. The greatest gift any child can receive is to spend their first 7 years with loving parents.

Of course, life is rarely perfect and many of us experience difficult childhoods, and this is all part of our journey. Our own wounds bring forth sweetness as we allow life to bring them to the surface for the purpose of healing.

Every time we heal a part of our heart, a little more of our greater being incarnates into the form. In time, we will come to manifest our higher purpose in life.

ALONENESS AND LONELINESS

Having a healthy SQ means entering into a profound relationship with your aloneness. The beauty and the ache of life is really played out through the seasons of our relationships. There are times when we are with someone, and times when we are alone. Often the nature of humanity is to long for the other side, so if you are alone you may find yourself at times longing for intimacy, and if you are with someone, you may long for more solitude and space. Your SQ speaks into this very human dilemma. Aloneness brings its own gifts, and one of these is an honouring of the sadness of life as well as its joy.

As you learn to contemplate life in more and more depth, you will come into touch with the inner fugue played by joy and sadness. There are times in life when we are called to enter into phases of deep melancholy. Sometimes there are reasons, and sometimes there are not. At such times we often ache with a kind of cosmic loneliness whose roots seem to go so far down into our depths, we wonder if we can ever be truly happy again. Such times can be difficult if we do not manage to maintain a sense of wonder and creativity in our lives. Without the creative process, there is a danger that we are pulled into the black hole of melancholy, which then sucks the life force away from us and leaves us feeling depressed. And once depression sets in, it can be very challenging to build up enough inner velocity to reemerge.

Almost all of life's greatest works of art, music, literature, and drama have emerged out of the genius of melancholy, or out of human beings who have allowed melancholy a deep place in their inner lives. If we are to rise to the peaks of consciousness, we must also hold a place for the nadir inside us. And this is a beautiful and vulnerable process.

Your SQ is a delicate balance of your IQ and your EQ, of your passion and your reason, of shadow and light, of intimacy and aloneness, of loss and love.

When you feel the call of your aloneness, then you must find a way to honour it, and creativity is the most vital and transformative way when you are following the Path of Love. Through creativity you maintain a state of communion with your fellow man. Others can see into your being, and take solace from the fact that there is something emerging there.

VENUS AND THE SOLAR PLEXUS

When you read the 55th Gene Key, you learn about the nature of the great inner transformation that humanity is poised to move through. This transformation involves a dynamic physiological shift in the way in which our solar plexus system works. Although we have always known that the feeling of love emerges through our chest area, the real source of this inner expansion is an open belly. The human body is a junction box of many dimensional fields, the majority of which lie beyond our ordinary senses. The teachings of the Corpus Christi that underpin the Gene Keys describe these many layers and fields of consciousness. There are rippling fields of quantum geometry that continually pulse in and out of our aura. This nexus of dimensional forces is an alchemical crucible for inner transformation.

As the Venus Stream awakens the next layer of humanity's greater awareness, a great inner healing is beginning within the entire human genetic matrix. This is a trans-genetic awakening that is occurring throughout the entire cosmos. This is again why your Profile is called 'hologenetic', because the process of hologenesis connects us into a vast cosmic shift that is holographic in nature. The Sphere of your SQ is calculated from a specific geometric position of the planet Venus when you are still in your mother's womb. It is here deep within your own process of genesis that the Venus Stream is emerging from. It involves the triggering of a pre-coded awakening sequence that begins before we are born.

The awakening sequence initiated by the Venus Stream of consciousness has a distinctly feminine quality. This obviously does not mean that it is only about women, however it is the living transmission of the holistic view of the universe. The masculine divides and analyses, whereas the feminine unifies and intuits. As this transmission sweeps through our human gene pools, it will change the way in which we operate. Our brain functioning will be transferred to a new centre of awareness that includes the solar plexus. Indeed our higher awareness is grounded in our belly. This means that the very process of human thinking will no longer understand itself as separate from life. The deep knowing of the solar plexus centre will inform our thinking. This in a sense brings an end to all questioning and questing. Once we know in our DNA that we are a living part of a vibrant whole, our whole motivation will change. Every decision we make will come from the holographic heart of life, rather than a brain that sees itself as a separate entity.

THE RING OF MATTER

In the Gene Keys revelation, every Gene Key belongs in a genetic family known as a 'codon ring'. The codon rings are very mysterious as they govern the way in which the collective karma of humanity is played out. The codon ring known as the 'Ring of Matter' contains 4 specific Gene Keys that control the awakening sequence through the phases of our childhood imprinting. The four Gene Keys of the Ring of Matter are the 57th, the 46th, the 18th, and the 48th. Each of these is a portal into the four phases of childhood development – our incarnation into matter. Contemplation on these Gene Keys in connection with your early development can be an illuminating experience. Of these Gene Keys, the 46th Gene Key controls the first 7 year cycle of our lives, and thus gives us a clue as to how our SQ really works.

The transformational path of the 46th Gene Key moves from Seriousness to Ecstasy, and it is the path of Delight. The Shadow of Seriousness falls across the face of every child at some point in their early years.

Because our adult role models are themselves deeply wounded beings, it is only a matter of time before we too become conditioned into the seriousness of the world. The Gift of Delight is the natural state of the young child inside each of us. It is the quality of wonder and optimism that comes from the knowing that we are not separate beings. Young children always have soft, open bellies, which means that they have soft, open hearts and smiles. They also tend to process difficult emotions with equanimity and purity. A young child can be sad but is rarely depressed.

The secret to the awakening of your SQ is how you deal with sadness and joy. Once you have overcome your need to try and escape sadness, you can develop a new relationship with it. Sadness and joy are a dance within us, and when we embrace and allow that dance, then something remarkable and marvellous occurs within us – the alchemy of ecstasy. Despite what you might think, ecstasy is not an extreme state of joy. It is the result of sadness and joy making love inside us. Ecstasy comes about naturally as we accept life utterly. It contains as much grief as it contains joy. It includes aloneness and intimacy, doubt and hope, mortality and eternity. Ecstasy is the highest expression of a fully functioning SQ. When you contemplate the Gene Key of your SQ and its line, think about how those qualities may one day lead you to a state of ecstasy.

THE COMING OF THE ECSTATICS, THE LAW OF LAUGHTER AND THE REBIRTH OF LOVE

The human solar plexus system is a highly complex neural net. As the ancients of all cultures have long known, it is the seat of our true power. Alchemically speaking, it is where we transform our emotions and desires. It is where the feminine essence of your astral body is sublimated into its higher counterpart in the Buddic body – the body of ecstasy. When we look back into history, we can see many men and women who rediscovered the power of their SQ and blazed a trail of love through the world. We call these people the Ecstatics.

The Ecstatics are a new race coming into the world. They come with a new kind of awareness rooted in the belly. We have always known that the belly is the place where laughter comes from. Laughter is like breath for the modern ecstatic. We do not even have to physically laugh, although that is exceptionally likely a great deal of the time. This is the kind of laughter that comes not from humour but from the deepest kind of compassion. Ecstatic laughter can be a glint in your eye, a soft, penetrating gaze, a poetic and considerate turn of phrase, or a playful poke in the ribs at the right moment. Laughter is the natural law of the future humanity. It is our primary human right to laugh at ourselves and at life. And this is not a cynical, sardonic laughter that draws joy from laughing at the plight of others. This is laughter that warms and opens. It may be at and with others, but this is laughter that expands consciousness rather than causing exclusion, humiliation, and isolation.

As your SQ opens and softens, your child's heart once more begins to beat in your breast. You will undergo a rebirth as your Siddhis begin to be catalysed. The awakening of your SQ requires that your awareness penetrates the patterns that were laid down in the first seven years of your life. This is a great transformational journey. As your awareness grows, so you will penetrate further and further back. Memories before the age of 3 are not stored in the mind but in the cellular memory of your solar plexus. You will remember the delight of these early years, and it will blend with the pain of your closing. Through this process you will come to see all human beings as wounded fellow travellers, and this will give you a compassionate edge in all your relationships. At this stage of your transformation, the unconditional love in your heart begins to burgeon, bringing you into the higher state known as Absorption.

ABSORPTION AND THE BIRTH POINT

In the teachings of the Corpus Christi, there are 3 major breakthroughs on the journey towards higher consciousness. The first breakthrough comes about as we learn the true nature of contemplation. To begin with, contemplation is a technique.

It begins with the mind as we consider and ponder our inner process. As we learn to see behind the low frequency unconscious beliefs we hold, another view opens up to us – our emotional world. When your awareness enters into your emotional patterns and becomes firmly entrenched there, you begin at last to transcend the desperation of your longing to escape life's pain. This in turn leads you into an even deeper stage of contemplation – physical contemplation. This is the deepest form of contemplation as your awareness enters into the genetic structure of the pattern itself. This is the place where awareness transforms us.

Physical contemplation is a breakthrough, because it occurs below your conscious awareness. At this stage your awareness is strong enough not to rush out of your body and project itself onto others as blame. It is also strong enough not to get caught in any repressive emotional pattern such as guilt or depression. As you practise the art of contemplation, you

169

may note these various stages as it becomes deeper inside you. At a certain point however, another breakthrough occurs. Contemplation gives way to the state of Absorption. Absorption is a mystical state when the love inside you begins to feed upon itself, leading to increasing states of prolonged ecstasy. Absorption happens as your awareness reaches the point of your birth.

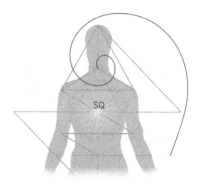

THE SACRED GEOMETRY OF THE SQ

When you overlay the Hologenetic Profile over a human body, you will find that the Sphere of your SQ is the very centre of your being, at the place of your heart. All the geometries and dimensions of your subtle bodies are centred in this point. It is this calculation of Venus, which gives its name to the whole Venus Sequence itself. Once awareness opens up in this place within your being, then you are in a sense reborn. Your journey is still not over, but from this moment on, your full awakening is guaranteed. Your Hologenetic Profile is calculated from the moment of your birth. This is a magical and symbolic moment, as it grounds you as a physical presence in the time/space continuum.

As your awareness travels back like the salmon to the source of its birth, so your mythology is realised in the world, and your whole Profile peels open from this point of breakthrough.

THE SIX LINES OF YOUR SQ

As you contemplate the 6 lines of the SQ, you should know that you are looking at qualities of consciousness that the developing child needs. These qualities never change throughout our lives. They dictate our journey of seeking and motivate our mythic identity.

They also happen to be universal themes that can be inspirational to us all. As with each Sphere, you are recommended to read and contemplate each of the 6 lines.

Line 1: Certainty (Rhythm and Routine)

When a child comes into the world, from the moment the birth cord is cut, they are seeking this quality – certainty. We enter the world with a sense that there is now something missing. In the womb it wasn't missing, because there we were completely connected into the floating oneness of it all. The 1st line is always asking these same fundamental questions: why am I here? what am I? The search for certainty is the epic human quest for answers to these deepest of questions. This is a cellular uncertainty that we carry from birth. If you have a 1st line SQ, then finding a sense of inner security will be your most fundamental issue in life. This deep genetic need for a sense of security will motivate your entire life.

Of course, where this search takes you is another matter. It can take us up or it can take us down.

What the developing child needs above all else is a strong sense of rhythm. Rhythm brings a sense of security, because it connects us into the cyclic forces of nature and the universe. The rhythm of the seasons, the rhythm of our heartbeat, the rhythm of our daily activities – all these things are an oasis for the young child. You might like to consider the rhythms of your early childhood, and whether they made you feel safe or uncertain. The young child is imprinted through repetition and routine. When we are older we may find such things boring or relentless, but to a child in their first 7 years there is nothing as important as a healthy life rhythm. If the young child is supported and buoyed by the healthy pulse of living rhythms, then when they mature they will always carry this profound cellular memory that all is well in the world, even when the opposite appears to be the case.

Our need for certainty can also take the route of fear. We can lock ourselves into routines that keep us from breathing and that throttle our creative spirit.

We can become unconsciously obsessed with finding certainty, perhaps through a will to power or through a self destructive tendency. We can fix our minds on certainty through a set of manufactured beliefs that keep us from being open-minded and flexible. We can become a victim of the details and drudgery of life, or we can become a workaholic and live in a state of denial. We seek these kinds of routines out of our deep fear of the uncertainty of life. If you have a 1st line SQ, you need to be aware that you will unconsciously seek certainty and security from others. This can put great pressure on your relationships. You need to look deeply into this habit of transferring your fear onto others. The only place you will ever find certainty is in your own heart.

As adults we continue to need rhythms in order to thrive. A life without natural rhythm is directionless and unable to support a process of maturing. Of course rhythms also change. Sometimes events occur that give birth to a completely new kind of rhythm.

If you have a 1st line SQ then such times can be really challenging for you, but they are also necessary. A healthy rhythm needs regular changes in tempo. The heart opens as you embrace the trials of your life and relationships and allow yourself to be transformed. Perhaps the most important rhythm of all is the changing beat of our evolution. Our dharma provides a rhythm that inspires us to stretch, grow, adapt, expand, excel, and ultimately flourish. How goes the rhythm of your awakening?

Line 2: Freedom (Wildness and Boundaries)

The 2nd line is always seeking freedom. You may recall the metaphor of your SQ as the yearning of the mythic traveller to come home. If you have a 2nd line SQ, then your home is freedom. You can see how each of these lines holds a truth for us all. All human beings yearn for freedom. Your line therefore places a stronger emphasis on this quality than all the others, and it also gives the Gene Key of your SQ a very particular flavour. When you look at the Gene Key of your SQ, think about it in terms of the quality you most need in order to feel free.

This is the spirit that lies behind all the 2nd line keynotes – passion, dance, posture, brilliance, courtesy – these are all themes that either involve or inspire freedom.

In the developing child this freedom is an essential ingredient in their early upbringing. The young child needs to be free to explore their surroundings. If they are too restricted or cosseted, then they will never experience life's natural boundaries. Of course this doesn't mean you let your child put his or her hand in the fire. But you might let him crawl up to it and feel it warm his skin. You will need to intervene if he looks like he is endangering himself, but it may also be that he will inherently figure it out for himself. This is the spirit that all children need – a healthy balance between freedom and boundaries. You can consider your own early upbringing – how was this balance? Was it lopsided in any way? Some parents do not give their children enough in the way of boundaries. Some parents simply neglect and ignore their children altogether. Many modern parents seem afraid to say no.

And of course there are those who fall on the other side – people who are so strict that the child is constantly unable to explore the world with a sense of freedom, but are always being punished simply for being the way they are.

If your boundaries as a child were lacking, then later in life it is possible that your life may lack a solid sense of direction. The imprinting of our SQ is so deeply structured into our physicality that it tends to radiate out into all areas of later life. This can also bring a lack of boundaries into our later relationships, or indeed it may illicit a reaction where we become too controlling. The general pattern of the 2nd line SQ in later life is frustration in their relationships. This frustration comes because the 2nd line SQ is wired to seek freedom, and yet they are also designed for one-to-one relationships. The 2nd line can be very intense because of this deep-seated need for freedom. Their dilemma is that they love intimacy, but still need to express the wildness of their true inner nature. This will involve some maturing!

The 2nd line will learn that true freedom is an inner state rather than an external requirement. You can be wild at heart and still deeply committed to another person, and you can be wild at heart and still live any kind of life, in any kind of environment.

The 2nd line SQ teaches us all a powerful lesson – that true love is inclusive. Love that depends upon a set of external conditions is not yet worthy of being called love. Our relationships can be a direct route towards inner freedom if we give ourselves to them 100 percent. Committed relationships offer us the ideal balance between boundaries and wildness. The relationship itself is the boundary. It provides the banks of the river, and the love is the wild, untameable river itself.

Within the relationship the flow of love will meet many obstacles, but over time as our hearts open and soften, the river slows down and matures, just like our love. As we evolve more fully, we begin to access the unconditional love that beckons us from the ocean itself. As the river widens to a delta, so our hearts come to realise that without those banks and those boundaries, we never would have reached this place of ineffable peace and unity.

Line 3: Pleasure (Adventure and Understanding)

If you have come this far along the Golden Path, you may be developing a good intuitive feeling for each of the 6 lines as their themes run on from sphere to sphere. It might not come as a surprise that the 3rd line at its core is therefore a lover of pleasure. This is the pleasure of life rather than pleasure as a distraction from life. The 3rd line is by nature adventurous, changeable, even quixotic. Such people are the buccaneers of the inner planes. As young children we float on the tides of life with a pleasure that is self evident. As adults we watch the young ones with a wistful eye, wishing perhaps that our lives could once again be that simple. To be able to draw pleasure from life is a rare and precious gift, and it is the great legacy of all 3rd lines. These people remind us why we are alive. Their ability to keep going when others have long since given up hope is also a bolster to us all in difficult times.

The developing child needs to feel from the people around him or her that life is indeed a joyous occasion. The child already feels this in every cell, but to have it confirmed by those around him reinforces the feeling, leading to a natural optimism that will stay with him for the rest of his life. Unfortunately many children receive the opposite impression – that life is primarily hard and miserable. This leads to a deep doubting of the life force itself, which over time may well become a pessimistic outlook that also stays with us for the

LOVE - A GUIDE TO YOUR VENUS SEQUENCE

rest of our adult life. This sense of pessimism may be lodged down in the depths of our being so that we do not even realise its existence. However, whenever we meet an obstacle in life we may give up on ourselves with startling ease.

The 3rd line is also vulnerable, perhaps more so than any of the other lines. It's interesting that the toughest can also be the most vulnerable. If you have a 3rd line SQ, then you need to reawaken the childlike spirit in your nature. You can stop taking your life so seriously. Life is a grand adventure, and you are the great anti-hero or anti-heroine. This means to say that your life brings you adventures and challenges that may surprise you or shock you, but your attitude towards the events of your life is everything. Can you let go of the past?

Can you dust yourself off, forgive and try again? Adults so often forget the essential in life. We are so busy we forget even to look out the windows at the sky, the trees, the gifts that lie littered all around us.

As a 3rd line SQ, you of all people are an ecstatic. To be an ecstatic means to suck the marrow out of life, to make the most of each day, and to learn to distinguish the essential from the inessential. What is essential to joy? Human relationships are a primary essential. The 3rd line SQ is here to learn the gift of understanding. Understanding another person takes time. It is neither linear nor logical. People are full of contradictions and idiosyncrasies. To love people we have to let go of our expectations and take them as they are. To understand someone you have to listen to their heart even beneath their suffering, and you have to let go of your personal agendas.

For a 3rd line to make a solid and lasting commitment to another person, it takes an act of utter dedication. It takes great courage and devotion to the path of heart, because the 3rd line is so used to running.

No matter which line you have or don't have, you can see how beautiful a thing your SQ is. It dictates your natural sense of spirituality – your connection to life through your heart. Natural spirituality may have nothing to do with any system or religious beliefs. Your SQ runs beneath the world of ideas and structures. It responds to life through living relationships – your relationship to the open air, to the sunshine, to those you love, to those you dislike. Your SQ allows for anything under the sun. It is the spirit of the eternal child within you. It is most definitely worthy of your deepest consideration and contemplation.

Line 4: Belonging (Kinship and Community)

If you have lived life to the fullest extent possible with a 4th line SQ then when you die, your funeral will be attended by thousands of people wishing to pay their respects. It won't necessarily be your life that is remembered - it will be you. In your life you will touch so many people. This is the fullest role of the human heart – to reach out and make the world a better place to live in.

Once again we must return to our childhood, and remember what it is like to see the world through those early eyes. The young child lives in a state of natural trust. No matter who you are or whatever your past, the young child sees you as innocent. The 4th line SQ is accepting of others in this way. Unlike the 3rd line however, the 4th line will have a very different life journey. The 4th line unconsciously seeks a home through community, whether that is a gang in downtown LA or a team in a modern business corporation. The 4th line SQ thrives on consistency of contact and trust.

When you contemplate your childhood, ask yourself whether you felt this sense of togetherness and community. Perhaps it was through your friendships or your extended family.

The modern nuclear family can be difficult for the 4th line SQ, which needs as wide a communal framework as possible in order for deep trust in humanity to evolve. Whatever your upbringing was like, as an adult you are likely to go on looking for that sense of belonging. One of the dangers of the 4th line is that it may get stuck in a community or group that is not actually nourishing, but out of fear it may stay with the familiar. If you have a 4th line SQ, then you will have many relationships that all fulfil different roles and nourish different aspects of your psyche. However, you needn't expect all these people to get along together!

The healthy, open-hearted 4th line SQ is likely to be very successful in the world in whatever they choose to do. This is because of the huge potential of their natural gift for networking. Being likeable is a most fortunate trait when it comes to business. Indeed, being likeable makes your life easier and more enjoyable in just about any sphere of life. When you contemplate the Gene Key of your SQ, consider these qualities as your primary networking Gifts. Also consider how the Shadow of the Gene Key of your SQ prevents your life from being so much easier and filled with grace. The 4th line is constantly searching for the place where they feel they belong. In their relationships this can cause friction, because they can place an unbalanced emphasis on their partner to fulfil their needs.

If you have a 4th line SQ, then you must learn that a sense of belonging really comes from having an open heart. The home that we are unconsciously seeking through our SQ is inside us. You may recall that the 4th line Purpose is about the breath. The 4th line SQ is a journey of deepening the breath. This cannot be forced through any external technique, but only comes about as we soften our hearts. As our breath moves deeper into the belly, so we become much calmer. The 4th line SQ has a most serene and relaxed countenance, which is why it is so easy to like them – because they have the gift of making you feel at home as well as making you feel like you belong. In this way the 4th line SQ is the epitome of a relaxed and welcoming heart and hearth.

Line 5: Mentoring (Role Models with Integrity)

The 5th line SQ is destined for greatness. The theme of life's true mythology is the victory of love over fear. Every time you see a 5th line in someone's Profile you are seeing an aspect of consciousness that has the capacity to exhibit great power in the world. If you have a 5th line in your Profile, you can contemplate how that quality might one day become a beacon for others, and at the Shadow frequency you can also contemplate how that quality could lead to a loss of power in some way. The 5th line SQ however conveys a spirit of awe, not as an arrogant quality to be flaunted, but as a quotient of the grand interconnectedness of all being. And the 5th line has the qualities necessary to translate this numinous view of life into everyday language so that it is accessible to all. This is the potential of the 5th line – to make love real in the world.

As a young child we all need role models to look up to. In our first 7 years when the physical body is paramount, these need to be living, breathing people that we have regular interaction with. Later on in our childhood, often our role models become mental and emotional in nature, and we project our longing onto an external hero or heroine with whom we feel a resonance. But in our early development cycle, the role model we look for is one who exudes love and wisdom.

Our primary role model during this phase is our mother, who will hopefully fulfil our ideal of unconditional love. There are also often other role models in our early years, and the 5th line in particular needs this. This can be a loving father, grandparent, uncle or aunt, or someone who shows a particular interest in you. This 'special' relationship may have a kind of mentor quality to it, as though the relationship is an oasis that you can always go to.

The role models in our early years become imprinted in our psyche as a kind of inner daemon, which we will carry with us throughout our childhood. A great deal therefore depends upon the integrity of the role model. With a 5th line SQ, you could take one of two directions in life – the journey of love or the journey of power.

If you take the latter, then you will consistently feel that you deserve more than you have, and the quest for wealth or fame or fortune may dominate your life over and above the quest for love. On the other hand, the journey towards love may also lead you to a position of power or authority, but with one great difference – you will use your position to serve the greater good, rather than to serve your own lack of self-love. The Shadow of the 5th line drives it to seek power in the external world, because they were not wholly nourished as children.

The beauty of a 5th line SQ is its practicality. It can use anything as a means of spreading goodwill. The healthy 5th line SQ radiates a combination of love and wisdom. If you have a 5th line, then in time you may become a role model or mentor for others younger than yourself. It is up to you to pass on those values and virtues to others. Of all the lines of the SQ, the 5th line has the capacity to spread the highest frequencies the furthest. You can contemplate the Siddhi of your SQ, and imagine how needed and powerful a quality that may be in our current world. Once you have caught the essence, you can go about the business of making it happen.

Line 6: Patience (Time and Space)

We complete our journey through the SQ with the 6th line and its primary theme of patience. The 6th line is the most mysterious and hidden of the lines. Like an iceberg, it carries the majority of its weight beneath the surface. There is a specific destiny written into every child that comes into the world. Your Hologenetic Profile gives a clue as to the nature of this higher purpose. As we journey through each of the 6 lines, we are seeing the universal themes that are then translated and filtered through the 64 Gene Keys – the codes that carry our mythic identities. We have seen repeatedly that the 6th line carries a vision into the world. In the case of the SQ, this is a vision that is always ahead of its time. People with a 6th line SQ are like the custodians of our common future. They have the potential to unify the rest of us. They carry a code that places all the other lines and their themes into a universal, holographic context.

The 6th line SQ is the most commonly misunderstood child. Unless they have an unusually sensitive and loving parent or parents, then these children may never get their deep needs met. Their deepest need is for time and space to develop without interference. These children may develop at a different pace from their peers. They may also display unusual characteristics. They need to be considered in a different way from other children. This is not because they are any more special than anyone else, but because the rhythm of their development is unusual and different. Later in their lives, people with a 6th line SQ may go off at all kinds of tangents in life. What such children need is the quality of patience from their parents and peers. Patience is a field of trust that instantly puts a young child at ease. In our modern world we often lack this timeless quality, because we have created a synthetic system that is insensitive to the incarnating child.

To be given time and space and to grow up with unworried parents is a precious gift! The 6th line SQ contains a living transmission of love that will one day emerge in the world if it is given enough time, space, and patience. If the 6th line is rushed, pushed, or pressured, then they may never move through the transformations that they need in life. It is easy for such people to give up on themselves and compromise their dreams in life. The greater dream always lives hidden in the hearts of these people – it is the dream of a better world. The paradox of the 6th line's dream is that they do not know how to enact it. They feel it always unless they succumb to the collective Shadow frequencies, but how to bring it into form?

The answer to the above question is patience! The dream will emerge in its own time, in its own way. The secret is not to interfere with your own process. You don't need to speed it up or slow it down. Nature knows best. As a 6th line SQ, you do not have to spend your life trying to understand everything. You may do that because you don't feel the depth inside yourself, so you must take heart and know that the answers are inside you. In time something extraordinary will emerge from you, as sure as the butterfly will emerge from the cocoon.

CONTEMPLATING YOUR SQ – THE ART OF PHYSICAL CONTEMPLATION

When you come to contemplate your SQ, you are bringing your attention to the heart of the Venus Sequence. You may be triggering a sleeping giant within! Represented by the archetype of Venus, your SQ is a hub of pure potentiality within your breast. As you bring your attention to this point, allow your contemplation to move much deeper into areas where the mind simply cannot follow. Even your emotions cannot follow you this deep down the well. This is the physical domain. Your body really does contain physical codes, and love is awakened as we activate those codes through deep contemplation on this Sphere. You can begin by thinking about the Gene Key of your SQ and its line. Then allow yourself to go deeper than the mind and turn your attention to the essence.

Consider the Shadow of the Gene Key of your SQ. Understand that it was not your fault that your childhood was not perfect. It was no one's fault. It was all a part of the plan. Out of adversity comes forth sweetness and great strength. Out of your SQ springs forth the gentle fire of your love. The purity of your heart is always present as an essence in your breast.

It emerges as your breath falls deeply into your belly, when you soften the muscles of your face into a natural smile, when you breathe into the sacred wound that you carry.

As your awareness comes more deeply into your body, and particularly into your belly, you will come into touch with your own deep well of suffering. On the other side of that suffering, just a hair's breath away is your love. We have to learn to hold both the pain and the love. We have to learn to be grateful for our life and for our relationships. Our relationships offer us the greatest path of transformation. You can always overcome a difficult childhood. That is the lesson that every relationship teaches us. When we view each relationship as a treasure, no matter how hard it is, then we are on track for triggering the great love inside. Physical contemplation makes the whole Golden Path so much easier. You no longer have to worry about understanding any of this knowledge. You just let it in. You allow it to percolate. You give it time. You breathe in the insights that inspire you, and you let go of your need to be anywhere other than where you are right now in this moment.

In the wonderful words of Mother Julian, who discovered the depths of her SQ:

All shall be well and all shall be well
and all manner of things shall be well.

11. THE PATHWAY OF REALISATION

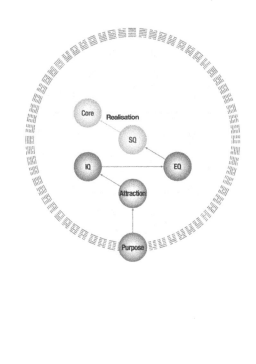

RETURNING TO THE ONE POINT

The transition from the Sphere of the SQ to the Core is no transition in time.

At this stage in our journey, the sequence itself is shown to be a limited way of viewing this transmission. Once you enter into the mystical state of Absorption, you are no longer in the hands of your ego or your sense of 'I'. There is a place within us where the forces of evolution meet the forces of involution. We call this place the 'One Point'. In the holographic universe, this point is located behind the navel. This place is a wormhole leading right into the heart of the universal consciousness. Words too begin to dissolve as they are drawn into this whirlpool of silence.

The Pathway of Realisation is like a lighthouse within us. From the moment we are born, it sends out its precious rays of remembrance. It waits for us to respond to its call, and only when we are ready does the process of Absorption begin. At a certain point in our evolution, we simply let go of all the structures that have pretended to hold up our life. We yield ourselves up to the mystery within, and we let it take a hold of us.

Before we were born, when we lay submerged within the womb, we lived through nine months of hologenesis. That is we moved through the process of Absorption in reverse. Emerging out of the void, we became progressively enrobed in the sheaths of matter as our tiny organs developed. In the womb it has been suggested that the various stages of foetal development mirror key archetypal phases in the evolutionary history of life on earth. We move through such 'hologenetic' phases from the moment we are conceived until the moment we are born. All phases form around the One Point, the umbilical nexus that provides the nourishment necessary for life to continue evolving.

THE ONE POINT

The One Point exists at a quantum level beyond the physical, observable plane, and it serves as a template for life to come into manifestation. It is the white hole through which light passes from the formless dimension to the plane of matter. It is where non being becomes being. It is an intriguing mystery that in order for our human evolution to attain its zenith, our consciousness must return down this same pathway, passing through the black hole of the One Point back into the realm of the formless. This is the true meaning of the Pathway of Realisation. It is also why words and language are no longer capable of capturing the essence of this experience. The experience itself is beyond words.

TEMPTATION AND DISTRACTION – THE RING OF TRIALS

Throughout the Gene Keys and the Golden Path, we have heard about the mystery of the 21 Codon Rings - specific groupings of Gene Keys chemically bonded together in genetic resonance. The breadth of the wisdom contained in the Codon Rings remains outside the scope of this book, but we can still glean a great deal of wisdom from them.

One Codon Ring in particular has a strong relevance to this Pathway of Realisation. This is the Ring of Trials, which consists of the 3 so-called 'stop codons' – the 33rd Gene Key, the 56th Gene Key, and the 12th Gene Key. The stop codons represent codes in our DNA that terminate processes of genetic replication, creating pauses or breaks in the process of protein building.

As archetypes, the 3 stop codons of the Ring of Trials represent a crux point in the evolution of human awareness. As we approach the Pathway of Realisation, we undergo a process of deep inner testing. Once we have opened up our SQ to its true potential, the currents of the higher frequencies begin to course through our being. We feel a new kind of power opening up inside us. The light of our genius opens up vistas of potential that we may have never dreamed of.

There is a delightful urge at this stage of our inner journey to try and hold on to the higher frequencies – and to follow their potential out into the world. The release of this great love inside us naturally urges us to want to be of service to the world and to others. It is possible to linger at this wonderful stage for the rest of our lives, and we can become a powerful force for good and change in the outer world. At least it may appear that way. The Ring of Trials sets us three mythical inner trials before we can continue to the very pinnacle of consciousness.

THE FIRST TRIAL – THE 33RD GENE KEY - REMEMBERING MINDFULNESS

At its lower frequencies the 33rd Gene Key is the Shadow of Forgetting. This is our first inner challenge. This Gene Key pursues us throughout our evolutionary journey. It opens in us as the Gift of Mindfulness – the knack we develop of allowing awareness to continually witness our own life. At the higher frequencies, our self-awareness is usually in an advanced stage of development. Awareness catalyses transformation, which is how we evolve in the first place. However, our awareness is tested at its deepest level once we begin to unlock the codes of our higher evolution.

It becomes all too easy to forget our inner journey and follow our love out into the world. There is a noble tendency at this stage to want to save the world in some way!

With Mindfulness all impulses are eventually shown for what they truly are. The impulse to serve others, while noble, can also be a distraction from continuing our inner journey to its true conclusion. This doesn't mean that the impulse to serve is wrong. It may be correct for us, but this is a classic stage in our evolution. Until our awareness has reached the Sphere of the Core, our true higher purpose cannot be revealed. The 33rd Gene Key tests, hones, and sharpens our mindfulness to its greatest extent. Each of the 3 Stop Codons of the Ring of Trials holds the potential to pause or halt our inner journey.

THE SECOND TRIAL – THE 56TH GENE KEY – THE DISTRACTION OF THE PERSONAL

Although we number the 3 trials of the Ring of Trials in a sequence, they are all themes that are interwoven with each other. The second test of our deep self-awareness comes via the 56th Gene Key, whose lower frequency is represented by the Shadow of Distraction. The final great transformation that occurs within us as we travel the Pathway of Realisation is the shift from the personal to the impersonal. The love released through our burgeoning SQ connects us to life and to others in ways that are genuinely wholesome and uplifting. As we experience the effects of the state of Absorption, our bodies can also experience frequent rushes of ecstasy and deep, unconditional love.

Once again we are tested by the urge to linger in the state of passion and beauty. Our heart sways in a poetic dance through the poles of pleasure and pain, as we come into greater acceptance of the beauty and sweetness of the Sacred Wound at the heart of all things. The 56th Gene Key can distract us with the riches of such an expansive state, and at a subtle level we can allow ourselves to rest in this stage. In the Eastern traditions, this stage of evolution is known as the 'Realm of the Gods'.

We soar and dip and dive in the romance of our lives, and we can develop a powerful connection to those around us – to those who naturally come to sip and taste the higher states that we are experiencing. Many people can be distracted at this stage by the urge to teach others and share their inner state.

We remain subtly attached to the world through our relationships and through the personal love that moves from our essence towards others.

The 56th Gift of Enrichment teaches us to draw the nutrients from each and every stage of our evolutionary journey. This is not about denial. We can enjoy every step along the path, and we are forgiven for wishing to linger in this beautiful space of expanding consciousness. However, we are still called to move deeper in awareness into the source of the bliss, into the core of the Sacred Wound itself. The 56th Siddhi of Intoxication teaches us to move beyond the ecstatic planes into the even deeper places of silence that lie within.

THE THIRD TRIAL – THE 12TH GENE KEY – THE VANITY OF THE SELF

The third and final trial we undergo as we pass through the portal of Realisation is the surrender of our separate identity. It is the symbolic surrender of our voice. As we enter through the many layers of the self, we begin to touch the essence inside us. Our awareness becomes ever-more focussed upon the One Point. This process is akin to a nuclear explosion. We keep focussing the lens of our awareness into this single hidden inner point within us, and as we do so, the energy of our being seems to grow in power and radiance. This gives us a sense of awesome power and one-pointedness. In time we become a blend of focussed compassion and limitless power.

Once again there is a deep temptation to linger at this point, feeling the wonder of the silence and the power of light coursing through us. This is the stage that the ancient traditions often named the 'lure of the siddhis'. We feel our potential as a messiah, and many gifts of the higher frequencies can be accessed at this stage. The Shadow of Vanity is our greatest test.

It will challenge the purity of our heart, as we are called upon to let go even of this penultimate phase of our journey. For only then does the final nuclear explosion occur. We enter the mystical Ring of Secrets – the mysterious 22nd Codon Ring. The 12th Gene Key is the only Gene Key which exists as a Ring within a Ring.

This is the final letting go, and the 12th Gene Key and its Siddhi of Purity offers us the greatest guidance of all – that no matter what happens, keep listening to the purity of your heart.

THE SEALING OF THE FIVE SENSES

The Pathway of Realisation is the archetypal return of our journey from birth to conception. The physiological architecture of our awareness is precisely laid down during the 3 Trimesters of pregnancy. This Pathway therefore involves a rewiring of the foundations of our awareness. We have seen from the trials above that we are called upon to let go of all of the frameworks that we have become accustomed to over the course of our lives - our attachment to pleasure, power, and identity. In the ancient traditions of the Tibetan and Taoist teachings, one of the highest formulae for attaining realisation or enlightenment involves a process known as the Sealing of the Five Senses. This phase in our spiritual development is a kind of 'grubbing out' of the very roots of our false awareness – through a purification of the way in which the brain uses the five senses.

In the ancient esoteric traditions, the five senses were often referred to as the 'five thieves' on account of their tendency to keep drawing our awareness back out into the world and away from our Core. As we approach realisation we undergo an organic process in which our awareness seals up these five doorways, thus preventing us from trying to escape reality through our attachments to the outer world. As we uproot these attachments, so each sense is purified of its conditioned functioning and is returned to its pure form. It is rather like rebooting your computer, and resetting it to its 'factory settings'!

SIGHT AND LIGHT – UNNAMING THE WORLD

The final and possibly most sophisticated sense to develop in the womb is the sense of sight. This is therefore the first perceptual attachment that undergoes transformation. In our 3rd Trimester we develop the ability to sense light through the lens of the eye.

It is through our sense of sight that we learned to name the things and people around us. As our awareness digs into our visual world, so we begin to let go of language. We come into increasingly deep spaces and pauses in which language and thinking cease. We may even look at the world from time to time without knowing what we are seeing. Our visual cortex is also linked deeply to our memory. When we see an object or person, they arise in our brain alongside a web of interconnected memories and ideas. Through the eye of realisation these memories remain intact, but are viewed as surface parameters rather than defining the object we are looking at. This enables us to see directly into the essence of a thing. This is a part of the cleansing of our awareness as we learn to see the world as it is, rather than seeing the world through the construct woven from our mental world view.

SOUND AND HARMONY – RE-INTERPRETING FREQUENCY

Our sense of hearing is developed enough by the end of the 2nd Trimester for us to take in and process auditory information. The most potent sound we are aware of is our mother's voice, but we also respond to many other sounds. In the 3rd Trimester we begin to recognise the patterns and intonations of language, and we become aware of the connection between tone and emotion. All the 5 senses are intimately linked into the development of our brain and central nervous system. Our brain therefore learns to distinguish and categorise sounds as patterns connected to our emotions. As our awareness travels further back into our past, we discover an inner space where all sound is simply taken in without any interpretation. Some have referred to this as the 'harmony of the spheres'.

It is a higher attunement to the layers of frequency that surround us, and as we enter into resonance with this higher harmony, we become deeply centred in the One Point – that holographic inner ear inside us that receives life as wave upon wave of being.

SMELL AND OTHERS – DE-PERSONALISING LIFE

Our sense of smell also comes online during the 2nd Trimester. The first aroma we take in is that of our mother, and for much of our lives we will unconsciously seek this early sense of comfort and familiarity. The whole history of our sense of smell is therefore about our relationships. We often overlook the impact that our sense of smell has on us. The world of smell is far subtler than we realise. We smell each other at the deepest level through pheromones – delicate aromas and hormones emitted by the body that we take in at an unconscious level. Our sense of smell guides our intuition. As our awareness moves into this unconscious world, we get to see the subtle attachments we follow as we are drawn to certain people, foods, places, and cultures throughout our lives.

Letting go of these attachments is a process of de-personalisation as we realise that we no longer need the security of the familiar, which carries a faint echo of the comforting smell of our mother.

TASTE AND STYLE –
SEEING BEYOND DIFFERENCES

As we travel through the various developmental stages of the foetus in the womb, we will see how the architecture of our senses are interwoven like building blocks. Our sense of taste for example is strongly linked to our sense of smell. But the physical senses also lead to a whole web of patterns and habits that follow us into our lives. Our sense of taste develops in the 2nd Trimester, as we absorb subtle sensations through the amniotic fluid. Through this we develop predispositions towards certain food types and flavours. But taste is about more than just which food we are drawn to. It underpins our sense of taste in the wider sense of the word – the smells, sounds, and images we are drawn to.

It is the foundation of our unique 'style' in the world. As our awareness reaches back into this phase of our early development, we see how certain genetic predispositions draw us towards certain people, places, and things. At this level, we see through the programming that makes us appear different.

This will not necessarily change our own habits and style, but it allows us to see the ordering principle that makes us feel like an individual.

TOUCH AND IDENTITY –
BEING WITHOUT MOVEMENT

The first sense to develop in the womb and therefore the final sense to transcend is our sense of touch. Our ability to sense through touch develops as early as the end of the 1st Trimester. We might re-state Descartes famous axiom as 'I touch therefore I am', because it is this earliest sense that allows us to differentiate our perceived sense of separateness in the world. Touch gives us an identity, and touch is linked to movement. Without movement we can lose our sense of touch and therefore our sense of identity. This is why those who have attained realisation have always done so through physical stillness or meditation. At a certain stage of our spiritual evolution, the state of Absorption becomes so all-embracing that we no longer have an urge to move, but spontaneously enter into prolonged states of physical stillness. It is in this stillness that our awareness finally ceases to be 'our' awareness, but is shown to be the connective tissue of consciousness itself. We rest in a state of pure being, beyond identity and meaning.

THE FLOWERING OF THE RAINBOW BODY

The process of sealing the 5 senses described above varies in subtlety and in its nuances and timing depending on each person. For some it may happen over an extended period of time, while for others it may even occur spontaneously in a thunderbolt flash from the heavens. There are no rules at this level of awareness. Realisation is a burgeoning of our fullest being.

In the allegory of the Venus Sequence, we have seen each of the Pathways and Spheres symbolically represented through the passage of water in nature. We begin with the underground water of the Pathway of Dharma, which flows upwards as a geyser through the Sphere of Attraction. This in turn becomes the spring of the IQ, the rushing rapids and alternating quiet pools of the Pathway of Intelligence, and the breakthrough of the flood in the Pathway of Love. In the Sphere of the SQ, the river metaphorically meets the ocean as we open our hearts in unconditional love. Here in the Pathway of Realisation our journey attains its final flowering as the rainbow – the symbolic transcendence.

Many cultures have described this process of the final flowering of our consciousness into the so-called Rainbow Body. In terms of our DNA, it seems to be a hidden higher programming function wired into every human being. In the Gene Keys Synthesis, it is referred to as the process of Embodiment, and it is described through the teachings of the Corpus Christi in the 22nd Gene Key. We tap into a universal energy pattern known as the 'torus'. The torus is a dynamic geometric representation of life itself. It describes an infinite process of energetic flowering from one dimension to another. This process is perpetual, because the energy within this model is able to feed off itself without any leakage, a process as yet inconceivable to modern physics. At the same time, the state of permanent unconditional love is also inconceivable to most people.

RAINBOW BODY TORUS

The Pathway of Realisation, like all the Pathways of the Venus Sequence, is a metaphor for an inner journey, and that journey takes us into the heart of our suffering. Unless we are willing to journey to this place, true realisation will remain a phantom and a dream to us. Before we even consider such a process, we must come into alignment with the Sacred Wound inside us and as we do so, we will come into a state of Individuation. The state of Individuation was described in the introduction to this book. It is a state of openness and vulnerability that is rooted in a deep Core Stability. Once we have become grounded in our Individuation, then this Pathway of Realisation opens us up to the potential of attaining another dimension of Core Stability – one in which our anchor shifts from our individuality and is transferred to the One Point – the holographic centre of the universe itself.

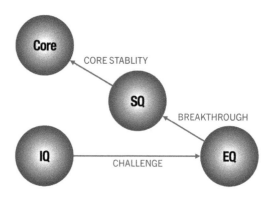

INTERDIMENSIONAL CORE STABILITY

12. THE SPHERE OF YOUR CORE

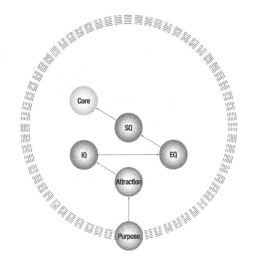

THE SPHERE OF YOUR CORE –
EMBRACING THE SACRED WOUND WITHIN

Now we arrive at the hologenetic centre of our being in this lifetime – the Sphere of your Core. In fact, each of the 11 Spheres of your Profile represents the centre of your being. Like a series of Russian dolls, each Sphere is a portal to a deeper level of being and purpose. In this sense it would be wrong to think of them as a linear sequence. They open within each other as our awareness reaches deeper into the nature of our being. The Sphere of your Core is the nexus of the Sacred Wound that you carry in this life. This wound connects you to all other human beings. It drives your evolution and is the very heart of your suffering. To bring full awareness into your core wound is to awaken fully to your limitless potential.

Some of us, quite understandably, do not like the idea of being wounded. Perhaps we feel healthy and happy most of the time, so why all this talk of suffering and wounding? Anyone who has looked inwardly at his or her own life will soon come into contact with their wound. Some people can feel it in a specific location within their body, while others know it as a deep sense of dissatisfaction or unease that lies beneath our conscious awareness. Some wear their wound openly due to an ailment or accident they may have had or even been born with. We all carry some kind of wounding – even the young child carries the Sacred Wound as a seed that will inevitably find its way into the world. One of the great revelations of the Venus Sequence is that our wounds are here to serve our higher purpose, so we need not flinch away from them.

Once you begin to come more deeply in touch with your specific wounding pattern, rather than getting weaker you will become inwardly stronger. Even though you may go through difficult and vulnerable periods, you will discover that the living transmission of the Venus Stream is most definitely on your side. Your consciousness will expand in relation to your willingness to embrace your wound. Up until this point in your Venus Sequence the emphasis on your wounding patterns has been on your relationships.

This is because the mirror of our relationships help bring awareness to the patterns most clearly and swiftly. However, as we dive into the deepest heart of the pattern, we move into the heart of our aloneness. This is a personal part of the journey whose implications lie deeper even than the outer love we have in the world. It takes a great deal of courage to bring your full awareness to this Sphere of the Core Wound.

THE WOUNDED HEALER – DNA TRANSMUTATION

In many cultures there is a mythic tradition known as the 'wounded healer'. This term may have first been coined by Carl Jung in describing his own journey of healing and integration, but the myth of the wounded healer or physician seems to be pervasive. In the Bible, Arthurian legends, Norse and Greek myth, Hebrew Lore, and many of the Eastern traditions, there is a tradition of a figure who having wrestled with their own vulnerability in some way, then becomes a healer and guide for others. Indeed this process of inner initiation is the mainstay of some of the oldest forms of wisdom on our planet – the path of shamanism. In the shamanic traditions, the apprentice shaman must take a series of initiatory journeys into the underworld of the unconscious. Here they will come into direct contact with the personification of their fears and their deepest wound. Having absorbed, embraced, and transformed their fears, the apprentice emerges and in time becomes the shaman – the wounded healer.

The revelation of the Gene Keys brings another dimension into this archetype of the wounded healer. As you will now realise, the Gene Keys are founded upon the premise that our higher evolution lies secreted in the coils of our living DNA. When the shaman therefore journeys into the underworld, he or she is really diving into the consciousness deep inside the physical body. In the inner journey your DNA represents the last stop before we move into the atomic structure, which connects us into the universal quantum field. This means that your DNA exists right on the threshold of universal consciousness.

It must be passed through before we can realise the peak of our spiritual evolution.

We know from genetic biology that the majority of our DNA seems to be unreadable, and therefore appears to serve no obvious purpose. This is known as 'non-coding' DNA or 'junk' DNA. This huge reservoir of information may well turn out to contain the history of our evolution. It is amazing what you can find out about a person when you rifle through their garbage! And such DNA may also contain the coded memories of the whole evolution of our species, and even the other streams of species that we have evolved from. If this is the case, then it would be true to say that we each contain the karmic hologenetic memories of our ancestors and their dreams and deeds. Such archetypal information lives deep within our unconscious, and it moves among our dreams.

In order for our awareness to penetrate the miasma of all this memory, we must each take the shaman's journey into the sacred wound – into the memory and the collective pain of our whole species. So much of our human past has been rooted in violence and fear. For millennia we have struggled to overcome the reptilian programming of our 'old' brain. And there are those who have won through. Our DNA also contains the echoes of our future consciousness. There have always been people who have braved the Shadow and taken the Path of Love. Some are remembered, but many are forgotten. In our ancestral DNA, we can therefore draw upon the strength of those ancestors who transcended their suffering and who were able to transmute this non-coding DNA. Such people also live inside us as allies, and their hearts are our hearts as we face the hardships that life throws at us.

THE ALCHEMY OF CREATIVITY

The archetype of the wounded healer expands beyond our many wisdom traditions. It is also a powerful part of the human creative process. One of the great poets of the past century, Antonio Machado, put it this way:

Last night as I was sleeping,
I dreamt—marvellous error!
that I had a beehive
here inside my heart.
And the golden bees
were making white combs
and sweet honey
from my old failures.

Most, if not all of our greatest artists, writers, musicians, composers, and crafts-people moved through periods of deep inner darkness. Out of this darkness and pain, they were able to transmute a large part of the Shadow DNA they were born with. It is a beautiful truth to contemplate that such inner darkness can lead to such outer light. Whenever you find yourself moving through a difficult period in your life, one of the healthiest ways of working through it is to engage in a creative project. The creative process is a dance along the banks of the unknown; therefore it is a natural outlet for an unknown inner process that cannot be helped by thinking or through any outer guidance. All works of genius emerge in spite of the mind, though they may be expressed through the mind.

The other health-giving aspect of true creativity is that it is in no way imitative. Whatever emerges through the creative process is fresh from the void. It is often as much of a surprise for the artist as it is for the audience. Creativity demands we become a patient witness to the magical secret forces of the universe. Patience and perseverance are the key qualities you will need to engage fully in the creative process. It can put us through a genuine initiation, as we struggle to bring forth the wordless dimension and dress it in the clothes of matter.

Of all the arts perhaps music is the favourite of the gods. The Sacred Wound within us can be instantly assuaged by the right intonation and cadence of sound. Sometimes a particular tune or song passes through us at a particular moment as though orchestrated by some winking cosmic director. With the right music we find we can open more deeply to the pain inside. It becomes more bearable and somehow more bittersweet. Music gets us breathing, remembering, and sometimes it gets us moving. The fact is that we are either a wounded victim or we make the decision to become the wounded healer. Music helps us forgive ourselves and others. Whether we are playing, singing, or simply listening, music oils the alchemy inside us, smoothing the way, softening the blows, rounding the sharp edges of our minds. As you enter more deeply into your own sacred wound, give yourself the gift of music.

DISEASE, ILLNESS, AND THE PHYSICAL BODY - 'PHYSICIAN, HEAL THYSELF'

One of the obvious places where we humans must confront the Sacred Wound face-to-face is through physical illness or disease. The moment we are faced with a serious illness, whether in our own body or through a friend or loved one falling ill, we enter a journey into that shamanic underworld mentioned earlier. Much will depend upon how we handle ourselves during the course of this journey. Will we be the wounded victim or the wounded healer? It is interesting to consider this question particularly when we are facing death, our own or another's. Sometimes physical healing does not occur. Sometimes perhaps it is not meant to occur. But there are other levels of healing. The ultimate healing comes through a thorough acceptance of death.

The Sphere of your Core holds the core programming for your suffering in this life. Even when your heart is fully open there remains a subtle clinging to this material plane. Our heart must stretch even further to embrace the fullness of our death, to accept the annihilation of the self. Physical illness can be a great leveller for us, stripping us down to the bare essentials of our being.

We must let go even of our heart's final longing to linger and help others. Ultimately, this is a plunge we can only take alone. In the Bible when Jesus spoke the words: 'Physician, heal thyself', he was alluding to this final surrender of the body into death. There comes a stage where we have to let go of everything, even our desire for the body to go on living. In saying these things, we are referring also to the mystical death, which we must pass through in order to reemerge as a fully realised being.

THE SHADOW

The Shadow of your Core Wound holds back a great deal of your hidden potential. The Sphere of your Core is a trigger point that lies on a genetic crossroads between your Venus Sequence and your Pearl Sequence. The Pearl, as you will learn, is about the true nature of prosperity. It is the practical arm of the Venus Sequence that flows out into your community and the world at large. Bringing your attention down into the Core and working to understand its impact in your life can therefore have startling effects in your outer life over a period of time. However, working deep in your Core in this way is not easy, as there are layers of karmic memory to burn through with your awareness. Sometimes it may seem that you are not getting anywhere, whereas in fact much of your progress is invisible to you. It is also vital not to become too tight when looking into your Shadows. Contrary to most people's beliefs, Shadow work is not such a heavy and unsettling task as you might think. It becomes heavy only if you allow yourself to forget the central point - to get in touch with the essence of your heart in the midst of difficulty. Even if you can only sense your heart as the tiniest tremor amidst a great backdrop of pain, that little seed is where your focus needs to be trained - not on the darkness but on the light. It is surprising how many people forget this simplest of truths, and become bogged down in wading through the sludge of the lower frequencies.

THE GIFT

Out of the Gift of your Core comes your greatest creative impulse. In the Activation Sequence, when we speak of higher life purpose we are referring to the creative potential of your genius. Your genius arises out of your Core as a process of personal transformation, the by-product of which is your outer work in the world. However, what we do in life is less important than who we are. We are here to learn to be ourselves. This is our primary gift to the world. To be yourself is to vibrate with the ideas of the cosmos inside you. It is to stand on a threshold quivering with excitement at the dream that is pressing to come through you. When you are living from your Core, no one can put you in a pigeon-hole, and no one can dissuade you from sharing your dream with the world. The Gift frequency is an expansion of consciousness that throws us into the delightful void of each and every day. When you live from your Core, then you always pay primary attention to your relationships. It doesn't matter how important you believe your work or your mission to be, it is as nothing compared to the treasure of your relationships and loved ones. This is the hallmark of a healthy life lived from the Gifts of your Core.

THE SIDDHI

The Siddhi of your Core carries the perfume of your essence. When the process of transformation through your Gift has manifested in your life, there follows a deep settling down inside you. The excitement of transformation and creativity subsides, the beauty and preciousness of your relationships mature, and a new essence begins to dawn within you. This is the light of consciousness. Consciousness is different from awareness. Awareness emerges out of the consciousness of a particular life form, but when that life form dies, the awareness dies with it. Consciousness however, remains. As your awareness is refined, so the mind and emotions quieten until the point when all that remains is the background of consciousness. The Siddhi of your Core gives you the flavour of the culmination of your evolutionary process as a state of realisation. The realisation however is not external to your humanity - rather it arises from your humanity.

This Siddhi comes right from the essence of your being. It is a fractal aspect of the whole in perfect resonance with the whole. Give yourself over to a period in which you bring awareness to the quality of this Siddhi over and over again. Sink into the heart of yourself and seek it with your full heart. If you do this, you will experience the true beating heart of the Venus Sequence, the Gene Keys, and the Golden Path, and you may never be the same again.

THE SIX LINES OF YOUR CORE

The 6 lines of your Core offer you a contemplation on the nature of collective transmutation. We each come into the world with a karmic genetic inheritance. Running beneath the personal trials and themes of our life is a deeper program wherein we are called upon to transmute aspects of the collective karma of humanity. In order for humankind to awaken to its true higher nature, we must first unlock these codes and transform them in our personal lives. When you are therefore contemplating the line of your Core Wound, you are taking on an aspect of human consciousness that is impersonal and has no root in your own personal life. Your Core Wound only has a root in your being in the sense that you are a far wider being than you probably realise.

THE SPHERE OF YOUR CORE (ALCHEMY)
CONCEPTION 0-9 MONTHS

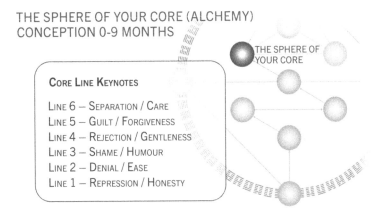

THE SPHERE OF YOUR CORE

CORE LINE KEYNOTES

LINE 6 — SEPARATION / CARE
LINE 5 — GUILT / FORGIVENESS
LINE 4 — REJECTION / GENTLENESS
LINE 3 — SHAME / HUMOUR
LINE 2 — DENIAL / EASE
LINE 1 — REPRESSION / HONESTY

Each of the 6 lines of the Sphere of the Core represent an archetypal aspect of the human wound. We each process one of these archetypes as a primary theme although our life inevitably involves all of them. As you contemplate your Core Wound and its healing opportunity, try to see it at work within all the other lines and Gene Keys of your profile. Rather than being an isolated unconscious theme, it lends each stage of your journey through the Venus Sequence a cosmic human context. In coming to the Sphere of your Core, you have reached the end of the rainbow, and even though there may be dragons beyond this point, they are the guardians of great inner treasure.

Line 1: Repression / Honesty

Repression is the first wound of all. At the collective level, repression refers to hidden, unexpressed fear. The Sacred Wound itself lies hidden within these very deep folds of our being. Few are those who are willing to look inwardly into the source of their suffering. The world provides so many distractions and reasons to keep the wound at bay. However, life will consistently provide us with invitations to examine the nature of our suffering – the greatest of these being death.

The human tendency in reaction to suffering is to breathe in a shallow manner and to close off our being to others and to the world. However, a more empowered response is to open your heart, and receive fully whatever life offers you. When you look at all 1st lines, you can always bear this in mind.

If you have a 1st line wound, then you may tend to internalise your suffering. The way you deal with suffering will likely be to keep it to yourself and to hold it in. For this reason, people with 1st line wounds may find it very challenging to express their innermost feelings with others. They can feel shut off in their own world, and often wonder if there is something wrong with them. So if you have a 1st line wound, then you are called upon to deal with the wound of repression. Contemplate the Gene Key you have in the Sphere of your Core and look at the Gift and Siddhi that is repressed behind this theme. Take a long and honest look at the Shadow of your core wound, and see it as an archetype that humanity has kept repressed for millennia.

Your role is to unlock this Shadow and transform it inside yourself. One way you can do this is through deep self-honesty.

Self-honesty is different from external honesty. In some respects, it is harder to be honest with yourself than it is with others. Look into your life. Allow yourself to feel the vibration of the Shadow of your Core. All you have to do is allow yourself to feel it, to become aware of it as a background frequency in your life. You do not have to fall victim to it or even be disturbed by it. The only disturbance comes from repressing it. You must allow the feeling in and realise that it cannot harm you. It is humanity that you can feel. It is the fear that drove our ancestors, and it is the same fear that drives the world today. All you are required to do is witness this fear in your life. It does not require that you express it or talk about it, although if you wish to that is also fine. As a 1st line Core, your style is to internalise things. So long as you do not lie to yourself, you will enter into a period of deep transformation as your awareness penetrates this Core Gene Key.

Line 2: Denial / Ease

The 2nd line carries the wound of denial. At the Shadow frequency, all 2nd lines live out different aspects of denial. We have seen how aggressive this line can sometimes be. When repression is finally expressed it usually emerges as anger, therefore the 2nd line is an exploration into the nature of anger. Unlike the 1st line, the 2nd line does not know how to keep things inside. Sooner or later they just burst out. Denial is always looking outwards. It cannot afford to look inwards, so it projects its suffering out into the world and usually onto others.

If you have a 2nd line wound, then your life is littered with reminders to look inwards at yourself, to take the leap and reach into the source of your suffering. Although others may try and harm you through their denial, the challenge is to let go of the conflict and draw the arrows of blame back inside yourself. People with 2nd line wounds often find that they cannot control their feelings, which at times threaten to overwhelm them and others. Look therefore at the Gift and Siddhi of the Gene Key of your Core for an answer to this.

You need never behave as though you are a victim of your wound. It is vital to remember that the deep pain you may feel is not a personal pain but the pain and denial of humanity. It connects you to others, to the reasons why we sometimes cannot contain our hurt, but project it outwardly onto others and often onto the innocent.

Contemplate the Shadow of your Core wound, and see how in denial you may be about its influence over your behaviour.

The 2nd line wound has a unique opportunity for profound healing. All you have to do is see your own denial. This may not be something you can achieve through effort, but through sustained contemplation on your own life, you will then come to see the pattern at work. Once you have seen it, you will feel an instant sense of liberation. Your great quality is ease. It is not as hard as your mind believes it will be to transform this Core pattern that keeps undermining your life. You will see it played out over and over again through your relationships. But your relationships can be so very different when you see through your denial. They can be so easy. Your life can have such a deep rhythm and sense of ease. The anger that sometimes wells up can be expressed in so many other creative ways. In time it will be completely transmuted into a deep and lasting compassion for all humanity.

Line 3: Shame / Humour

As the cosmic wound comes deeper into manifestation, we move from repression to denial to shame. Once we have emerged from our denial and looked deeply into our true nature, we will feel our shame. We might begin to think: how could we be so blind? How could we treat each other and the world in such a way? We all hold the great reservoir of shame inside our DNA. We each contain all the fractal aspects of the Sacred Wound. Shame is born out of our self-loathing. We do not like to look inwardly and see how deeply we are wounded, so we try to run and escape our shame. But no matter how far we run, our shame will always come with us. Often people think of shame as a feeling they would rather avoid, which is understandable. But shame also makes us human. Although it may be uncomfortable, it is the beginning of the process of learning to accept what we are.

If you have a 3rd line wound, then you will use life as an excuse to deflect the pain you feel. Unlike the 2nd line, which will engage the wound by projecting it, the 3rd line will just keep itself so busy that they will never allow themselves time to realise what they really feel. Shame will make you believe at a deep level that you are unworthy, and thus you may well spend all your energy trying to prove to yourself and the world that you are worthy. Many 3rd line people are quite obsessive in how they approach life – they may spend their days chasing their own tail or end up being a workaholic. All of this makes the 3rd line very difficult to relate with at a deeper level. At least the 2nd line will shout at you! But the 3rd line will never stay around long enough for you to get to know their vulnerable side. If you have a 3rd line, you must slow down long enough to get in touch with your feelings of unworthiness. You don't need to understand these feelings.

They are shared by almost every human being alive. You simply need to let someone you love see all of you, naked in your shame.

Contemplate the Gene Key and the Shadow of your Core in the light of the above, and remember that the great gift of the 3rd line is humour. This is not the surface humour that the 3rd line may also use at times to cover their true feelings. This is the humour that wells up from a deep intimacy with your own being. Yours is the humour that comes from a wondrous mixture of self-love and integrated vulnerability. When you can laugh at yourself and your many faults and gifts with compassionate understanding, then you have begun the fulfilling journey of transforming the shame of humanity.

Line 4: Rejection / Gentleness

The 4th line core wound is about rejection and abandonment. It is important to note here that each of these wounds are themes that we will meet in our lives. Sometimes the manifestation of the particular wound comes towards you from another person. This is why our relationships can be so difficult at times. If for example, you have a 4th line wound then perhaps as a child you may find yourself on the receiving end of this theme of rejection. The wound itself already exists inside you since it was imprinted before you were even born, but it waits for the external trigger in the world before it is actively engaged in your life. This 4th line wound is all about armour. Because we fear rejection, we learn to armour our hearts against such deep-seated pain. Most of us have experiences in our teens or twenties of some kind of heartbreak. Rejection is thus a universal human fear.

If you have a 4th line wound, then the likelihood is that you may reject another before they reject you. Rejection can be a very subtle thing. It can be conveyed through tone or body language in an instant. It often manifests as meanness. Often you are not even aware that you have pushed someone away until you see their reaction. All rejection stems from a lack of self love.

We fear that we can be hurt by another, whereas in reality it is we who are responsible for keeping our heart open. When you contemplate the Gene Key of your Core, you can consider the Shadow in the light of this fear of abandonment. The Shadow theme is intimately linked to your willingness to face your fear of being rejected by another. Contemplate the Gift and Siddhi of your Core at the same time and see what qualities you will need to uproot this deep fear.

The 4th line will often wear their fear as a subtle tension that spreads across their chest area. Many people with the 4th line wound may even have forgotten what it feels like to live without this tension. When the heart softens, an unaccountable joy wells up in our breast. This softening is the 4th line's speciality. Your great gift is gentleness. You will have to learn how to be gentle with yourself when you feel hurt, and therefore how to be gentle with others when they feel hurt or threatened. We must remember that these wounds are universal to all humans. We all know that feeling of tightness across the chest. The more adept you become at melting your own armour, then the easier you will find your relationships. You will no longer be a victim of someone else's need to push you away, and if someone happens to be cruel to you, you have the instant means of disarming that reactive hurt inside yourself. In time this will make you an extraordinary envoy of the power of love through gentleness.

Line 5: Guilt / Forgiveness

The 5th line often seems to be the most complicated of the 6 lines in terms of its Shadow patterns. Ironically the 5th line hates things to be complicated! They are the great lovers of the practical and the simple. At the Shadow frequency however, the 5th line is responsible for holding all the guilt in the world. Although guilt as a pattern sounds similar to shame, they are very different expressions of human fear. The 3rd line tries to escape the wound through activity, whereas the 5th line filters their wound through the theme of power. The Shadow of the 5th line does not allow people to have a peaceful relationship for long.

They feel a huge pressure from others to be a certain way and whether they compromise their own truth to be someone they are not, or whether they react by being the opposite, in both scenarios they end up feeling bad about themselves.

Such patterns in relationships breed deep resentments that tend to fester and also lead to power struggles. The Shadow pattern of the 5th line feeds off power struggles. It learns to manipulate others through guilt often without even realising it. As a collective theme carried in our DNA, guilt forces us into situations that we inevitably regret, making our lives more complicated at every level. Many 5th lines end up giving up on relationships altogether, and then they have to live with the guilt of their past still somewhere inside them, or their resentment of another becomes so great that they are unable to move on with their lives. If you have a 5th line core wound, it is unlikely that you will ever work out your relationships at a mental level. The complexity of the 5th line pattern will always confuse you. However, there is a very simple way out for you.

When you begin to contemplate the Shadow of the Gene Key of your Core, you simply need to feel the vibration of this quality of fear in your body. Your awareness of this will certainly make you feel vulnerable, but it needn't make you feel weak. You are not a victim of this fear. It is not even your fear. It belongs to humanity, and your role is to transmute it through the power of forgiveness. Over and over in your life you will be presented with the opportunity to forgive others for deeds that you may consider unforgivable. You must learn to see that all humans are driven by these unconscious core wound patterns. This does not validate certain Shadow behaviour, but it does allow us room for forgiveness. As you learn to forgive others, you are really forgiving aspects of your greater self. Look at the higher qualities of the Gene Key of your core wound. See what rewards lie on the other side of forgiveness. Refracted through a healthy 5th line, these are qualities that can reach out far and wide into the world. However, if you continue to hold onto resentments, then you are only limiting your own capacity for love and joy. This is as practical a teaching as you will ever come across in your life!

Line 6: Separation / Care

The 6th line wound epitomises the dilemma of our current human awareness. Through our mind, we experience ourselves as separate from existence. Our current awareness is mostly localised in the brain and identifies itself with the body and its related physiological and psychological functions. A part of the healing of our collective wound must therefore be to evolve a new system of awareness allowing us to experience an unbroken consciousness that is one with everything. The 6th line wound of separation is the most recent aspect of the Sacred Wound to develop, just as the 1st line wound of repression was its earliest expression. The 6th line therefore stands aloof from all the other lines, as though cut off completely from its true source. In order to heal, the 6th line has to become aware of its aloof sense of separation, and this is quite a process.

If you have a 6th line core wound, then you may already identify with the above paragraph. If you do not, then either your core wound is one of the other 5 lines, or you may be living inside a mental framework that you evolved as a very young child in order to cope with the world. The 6th line is hyper-sensitive as a child, and they are therefore easily misunderstood. The 6th line wound carries the potential genetic mutation of awareness itself, which means that such children may appear different from others.

Ideally such children need to be given space and time to develop in their own particular direction, without any external pressure. However because of the way society is structured, these children soon become homogenised and their special sensitivity falls dormant. If you have a 6th line wound, then your journey of healing will involve the reawakening of these early gifts. When you contemplate the Shadow of your core wound, you will see the particular vibration that you took on as a child.

The reawakening of the 6th line wound takes time. There is no fast-track method. Many 6th line people set off on a profound spiritual search later in life, in order to try and locate these Gifts and Siddhis that they experienced as a very young child.

Aloneness can also be a strong theme for you if you are a 6th line, and this can make relationships quite challenging. You may sometimes feel as though you are somehow locked out of the world that everyone else inhabits. You need to see that you are not a victim of the system or of anyone else's mistakes.

You alone can bring yourself back. You alone must learn to include yourself once again in the world.

For the 6th line this is a long and fulfilling journey of self-care. It is your heart that must be rekindled so that you begin once again to care about the world and the people around you. When you care enough, then you will begin to find yourself feeling more and more alive once again. As you learn to care for the world, the planet, and above all yourself, you will see that you have so much to give. Instead of being hidden away in some backwater away from all the action, you will take your place at the centre of the grand transformation that is coming to our planet.

CONTEMPLATING YOUR CORE – SEEING THE SACRED WOUND EVERYWHERE

When you contemplate the 6 lines of the Sacred Wound in all relationships, and especially in your own, you may begin to see how each wound interacts with another. The wound feeds off interaction. Guilt provokes shame, denial causes repression, separation fuels rejection. You can combine and recombine these 6 aspects in all manner of ways.

When you also bring in the 64 Gene Keys and their Shadows, you will see the whole panoply of pain that underpins human relationships. Of course our relationships are not always full of pain. They are a blend of Shadow, Gift, and sometimes even Siddhi. Our lives are lived as a dance of consciousness swinging between these archetypal poles.

The key to transformation is awareness. As we become aware of the Shadow patterns at play within our relationships, right down to this deepest level, so we loosen the hold that those patterns have on us. When you begin to contemplate the 6 lines of the Core Wound, you can watch your life for the signs of their qualities.

You can soon see them at work in the relationships and dramas of the people you know. You can even see them played out as fantasies in the great stories, novels, and films of all cultures. Perhaps you may also see how entrenched the Sacred Wound is in our DNA. We have become quite addicted to it as a cultural norm.

It is also quite unnecessary to know people's birth times and profiles in order to see the 6 lines of the Sacred Wound at work in the world. In fact it is far better that you learn to see the wound without any external reference. These 6 lines are frequency codes embedded in human DNA. The more deeply you see them, the easier it will be to understand them and accept them. The final step is to embrace the Sacred Wound fully inside yourself, and then you will feel a deep almost overwhelming sense of compassion for humanity and for the plight we find ourselves in. This wisdom of the Venus Sequence comes at a time where change is in the air, when finally we can begin to transmute these ancient patterns of inner conflict between the sexes – the patterns symbolised by Mars and Venus, God of War and Goddess of Love.

THE SATURN SEQUENCE AND THE RACIAL AND COSMIC WOUND

This next stream of information continues our deep contemplation of the theme of the Sacred Wound, but instead of viewing it as a theme embedded within the individual, we now consider it as a collective phenomenon operating through vast gene pools and entire civilisations. We can continue to use the 6 lines as a structure for viewing such themes, but they are no longer practical for us through the Hologenetic Profile. Where this knowledge becomes useful is in widening our contemplation to encompass a global genetic program that has shaped human civilisation throughout history. Such a view can be dazzling both to our mind and heart as we open ourselves even wider to take in the scope of this Divine plan.

Back in 2004 when I received the Venus Stream at the same time as the planet Venus was transiting the sun, I experienced such a heightened state of consciousness that I found myself reeling from the understandings that were coursing through my body. Towards the end of my experience, as I was coming down from the higher frequencies, I received a final burst from the heart of the transmission - a kind of afterthought from the gods. I called this the Saturn Sequence, because it has a different energy signature that is tied to the planet Saturn and its geometric revolutions around the sun in relation to the earth.

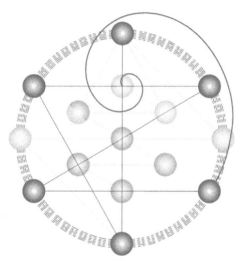

THE SATURN SEQUENCE

The Saturn Sequence shows us how personal transformation has a knock-on effect at a collective level, re-imprinting our gene pool with a higher frequency that will be passed on to our children and their children. To begin with, the Saturn Sequence can also seem quite shocking, as we see the fractal splitting open of the Sacred Wound into its collective Shadow themes, our tribal and racial wounds, and even our planetary and mythic wounds.

As you contemplate this information it's important to keep an open mind and heart, as you realise how your personal inner work can reach out and have a very real effect on many of the horrific global themes we see around the world today.

THE 6 LINES AS COLLECTIVE WOUND PATTERNS

In the original I Ching (as in the base pairs of our genetics), the 6 pairings are arranged as three sets of couplets (they are colour-coded below). The 1st line always relates to the 4th line, the 2nd line to the 5th line, and the 3rd line to the 6th line. When we look into these relationships, we can therefore see three basic dynamics at work.

THE 6 RACIAL WOUNDS

LINE	SHADOW STATE	SHEMA D O W
LINE 6	ANNHILATION	INDIFFERENCE
LINE 5	DELUSION	TYRANNY
LINE 4	HATRED	COLONISATION
LINE 3	PANIC	MIGRATION
LINE 2	RAGE	VIOLATION
LINE 1	TERROR	INVASION

Line 1: Terror / Invasion

At a racial level the 1st line becomes the theme of terror and the threat of invasion. Every 1st line carries this fear deep within its core. All the 1st lines throughout the gene pool imprint us through our ancestral memory with this primal fear. At a tribal level, this is the terror of having one's family and entire genetic line wiped out by another tribe. When you contemplate the 1st line in the light of your own Venus Sequence, you can see how this fear can lead to the 1st line's tendency to repress such a deep fear. All 1st lines fear a force that comes from the outside and threatens their security and stability. Out of this fear also comes the potential for the 1st line to become the invader itself, to make the preemptive strike and go out to conquer other lands and tribes.

Line 2: Rage / Violation

The 2nd line carries the rage of the generations inside itself. At a racial level this rage leads to the theme of violation. It is that part of human nature that can commit atrocious and violent deeds.

The ancestral anguish present in the 2nd line also emerges out of the grief that comes from having witnessed the violation of that which you love, whether that is your home, your loved ones, or your personal freedom and integrity. The rage present in the racial memory of human DNA makes human beings blind to personal responsibility. When you contemplate any 2nd lines you may have, you can always bear in mind its collective Shadow - this terrible racial pain that believes its only outlet is violence.

Line 3: Panic / Migration

We have seen the 3rd line's tendency to try and escape its own pain. It is the most dynamic and excitable of all the lines. As a collective Shadow frequency, the 3rd line emerges as panic. Panic is a collective reaction that can sweep through a gene pool like an infectious disease. It is usually a reaction to the patterns of the first two lines - the threat of invasion and/or violation. The 3rd line is all about movement and change. It has driven human beings for millennia. War, disease, famine - all engender panic to spread through a gene pool, and often this leads to a mass migration as that gene pool is uprooted. If you have a 3rd line, consider how you might resonate with this restless, relentless, homeless, frenetic aspect of the Sacred Wound.

Line 4: Hatred - Colonisation

The 4th line creates a dynamic with the 1st line. Invasion often leads to colonisation. We may recall that the theme of the 4th line is the social realm. At the Shadow frequency, this becomes the imposition of one set of genes upon another race. The 4th line is the source of racial hatred coming from the tension between both the invader and the victim.

Nonetheless, such global themes are constantly at play within the world even today. Contemplate your own 4th lines, and know they are capable of such contempt and coldness when you or those you love feel deeply threatened. Every 4th line is essentially looking for some sphere to colonise, whether that be philosophical, social, or in the case of the collective Shadow, racial.

Line 5: Delusion - Tyranny

The 5th line Shadow rules by keeping you under its thrall. Being deluded itself, it can make you believe in anything as long as you can be kept in the dark. And as the master of manipulation, the 5th line Shadow can pull the wool over the eyes of an entire gene pool. Human history is littered with such examples of charismatic and terrible leaders or philosophies that cast the Shadow of tyranny over a whole race of innocent beings. Beneath the 5th line's tyrannical agenda is usually a deep-seated 2nd line rage at being violated in some way in the past. When you look at your own 5th lines, you can perhaps see this behaviour written in microcosmic form. Through your willingness to delude yourself, you allow yourself to be victim of someone else or something else. Of course, the greatest tyrant of all is often the human mind.

Line 6: Indifference - Annihilation

The most dangerous of all the aspects of the Sacred Wound is the 6th line with its collective theme of indifference. It is dangerous only in the sense that it is furthest from being humane. We know the 6th line Shadow as being cut off, even discarnate, and here at the collective level it takes on a chilling flavour. Throughout history we see evidence of this indifference through the barbaric persecution of certain tribes or races. It is one thing to take over another society by force or even manipulate it for your own personal benefit. The 6th line however is an energy that will settle for nothing less than the annihilation of a whole gene pool. All 6th lines have the potential for such indifference at the Shadow frequency. It is this that provokes the 3rd line panic and the urge to flee and migrate to new and safer lands.

THE 6 PLANETARY AND MYTHIC WOUNDS
Line 6 - Indifference
Line 5 - War
Line 4 - Poverty
Line 3 - Greed
Line 2 - Violence
Line 1 - Disease

Travelling even deeper into the nexus of the human Sacred Wound, we come to the planetary perspective. At this level we are really looking at the evolution of human awareness as it tries to realise and remember its true nature. The splitting of life at the Big Bang into yin and yang, form and energy, male and female gave rise to an exhaustive evolutionary effort to come back into unity. Our planet Gaia provides consciousness with the arena for this extraordinary program to play itself out. The human being contains the full spectrum of genetic possibility, from the Shadow to the Siddhi, and our muse is suffering itself. It is our suffering that shows us most clearly where we are on the spectrum. Are we victims of our own low frequency programming? Or can we transmute that suffering, both individually and as a collective, and activate the higher frequencies embedded in our DNA?

Our dream of heaven on earth is a direct intuitive sensing of this higher possibility.

THE 3 PLANETARY WOUND DYNAMICS

Lines 1 and 4: Disease and Poverty

The 1st line always holds the key to the whole process. Fear is our disease. Fear is so deeply embedded into our ancestral memory that it will take a huge collective effort to transmute it. At the purely physical level, fear is expressed as disease. Every illness offers us the potential for an inner cleansing and transformation. If there were no fear, then there would be no illness. We have lived with fear for so long that we cannot even conceive of life without it.

Disease and illness is therefore a great opportunity for healing ourselves - not even necessarily at the physical level, but at the deepest level of the separate self.

At the social level of the 4th line, fear is expressed through poverty. We fear not having enough, so we are unable to open our hearts to those outside our gene pool. For most people, it is already a challenge to open one's heart even within one's gene pool. Poverty is a yardstick of how we are doing as a species. Our outer geo-political struggles are a metaphor for the deeper poverty we feel inside. We have not learned to touch and find our inner essence, so we are unable to trust in life itself. We have vast inner wealth at the core of our being, and until enough people have realised this, there will always be poverty on our planet.

Lines 3 and 5: Violence and War

It is easy to see the wound dynamic between the 2nd line and the 5th line. Violence towards oneself in the 2nd line manifests as war among the collective in the 5th line. Our fundamental violent tendencies are a hugely misshapen version of our passion for life. The 2nd line Shadow shows what happens to fear when it is released from its repressive state - it floods our endocrine system activating the oldest parts of our brain, and we become capable of killing. This is not even killing to survive, but killing as a way of releasing the rage and our self hatred. Violence occurs in microcosmic form every time you close off from your own inner essence and forget your true nature as love.

The 5th line represents the explosion of the 2nd line theme of violence into a collective form. Our planet has been wracked by wars since our earliest days when we began to form into tribes. Wars are usually the result of the personal violent agendas of certain individual leaders. The 5th line can lead us to peace or it can lead us to war. It is because we do not honour our own self-esteem that we allow and choose leaders who lead us deeper into the Shadow frequencies.

One day when enough individuals have realised their true nature, we may each become leaders through following our own higher purpose. Then we may finally see an end to war.

Lines 3 and 6 - Greed and Indifference

The 3rd line always seeks an escape from its own inner shame. At a collective level this becomes greed. Greed is an addiction. It is the very root of addiction. We feel empty inside so we try endlessly to fill that void by taking from the outer world in some way. In the modern world we can see how collective greed plays out through the great monopolies of the business world. It is based on the same sense of inner panic and restlessness that we saw with the racial wound. Money is the symbol of our greed. It is not that money is bad, but it provides us with the yardstick for self responsibility. One day the world may even be healed by the balanced use of the world economy.

We have already met indifference when we looked into the Core Wound. At a collective level, the greatest challenge remains the same - it is indifference. You can see here the relationship between greed and indifference. Indifference underpins all of the 6 lines at their Shadow frequency. Indifference epitomises everything that is asleep in human beings. On an individual level, only a very few of us have awoken to our true nature. Others are gradually discovering how to bring feeling back into their hearts, but at a collective level we remain mostly indifferent to our nature, our plight, and our future.

THE OPENING OF THE SEVEN SEALS
AND THE GREAT CHANGE

Having read the above I hope you are feeling more expanded rather than depressed. The Sacred Wound is the driving force of our evolution. When you look at the world from this higher perspective, it can open your heart fully to receive the suffering of our world. We are called upon to accept not only ourselves but also our greater body. The human being has an extraordinary capacity for intelligence.

We have vast possibilities hiding in our DNA that lie completely untapped. The other side of the Saturn Sequence concerns the unravelling and healing of the Sacred Wound. When we look at this knowledge from the evolutionary perspective, it does indeed seem daunting.

There is however another way of viewing the Sacred Wound. This is from the perspective of Involution. Involution concerns Grace - a force beyond our comprehension. Grace presupposes that not only are we seeking the higher frequencies, but that they are also seeking us. Everything in the cosmos seeks its opposite. This means that there will always be points in the story where breakthroughs occur. A breakthrough comes when the higher forces finally descend into the lower realms and vice versa. No one can predict when these events will happen, but they have always happened and will continue to happen!

From a global perspective, the Gene Keys carry the transmission of Grace and as you open to the possibilities of your Siddhis, you prepare the ground for a quantum leap. The more people that do this, the greater the collective leap will be. We live in the time of the 'Great Change' - a precious time when a great breakthrough is in the air. The Gene Keys prophesies that humanity will actually mutate its own genetic code in order to develop a new kind of awareness system. This new awareness will then allow us to transcend the mind and directly experience our unity with all things. However, this breakthrough is unlikely to occur overnight. It will likely change us gradually, from within, and as we change at the core, so in time we will also change externally. Our scientific understanding must also grow to encompass the holographic truth of our origins, and as a result the structure of our civilisation must change radically.

When you read the 22nd Gene Key, you will come to a teaching known as the Seven Seals. This teaching concerns the way in which the currents of Grace will gradually bring healing to the collective Sacred Wound. Certain Siddhis in the human genome, when activated collectively, will heal specific patterns in human DNA. For example, the 63rd Siddhi, which is about the embodiment of Truth, is the Siddhi that will finally bring an end to the 6th line wound of indifference. Once you know that you are all things and are connected to all beings, it is no longer possible to be indifferent. Once the candle is lit, the darkness is gone. The teaching of the Seven Seals may seem fantastical, as may the Siddhis themselves, but they are the counterforce to the Shadow frequency.

Where there is darkness, there is also light. The light lives within the darkness, and one day when we realise this, then the darkness will no longer be perceived as darkness, but as the harbour of the limitless light that lies within.

EMBRACING YOUR CORE WOUND

Perhaps you can see and feel how deep a transmission this Venus Sequence contains. At the heart of it lies your Core Wound. Bring your particular attention to the Shadow, Gift, and Siddhi of your Core. Out of this wound will pour forth sweetness. It is your wound that makes you human. The final stage in opening our hearts is to learn how to let our love interface with the human world. Human love is down-to-earth, practical, caring, and selfless. Human love respects boundaries, and is willing to operate within limitations even though it is unlimited. Thus it is through our wound that love comes to earth. It requires the qualities of care and harmlessness. It is about seeing all the expressions of love in all their rainbow colours and accepting them utterly.

All love makes us grow. It makes us human and invites us to continuously surrender our smaller self to our greater Self. Each relationship in our life offers us this marvellous opportunity. When you live within your Core, you rarely need to leave a relationship because you no longer dream of love 'out there'. You have found love as a source inside and you embody it, so you are willing to stay with what life brings to you. You accept your karma. You become mature. You are at peace. This is the essence of the Venus Sequence – simply to be at peace.

13. INTEGRATING THE VENUS SEQUENCE INTO YOUR LIFE

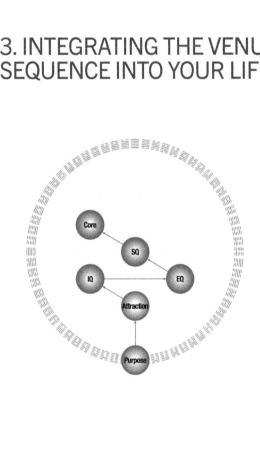

CONTEMPLATING AND WORKING WITH YOUR VENUS SEQUENCE

Having reached the Core of your Profile, you now have all the ingredients necessary for a powerful transformation in your life. Opening your heart is an ongoing process requiring a constant refining of your awareness. There are many ways of working with your Venus Sequence, but to give it the time it needs to bring about lasting changes, it may be useful to give yourself a structure to follow. You might like to return to the beginning and give yourself one week or perhaps even one month to contemplate each Sphere of your Venus Sequence. You can do this alone as an inner process or together with another person or group.

The Gene Keys Synthesis is an open system without levels or trainings or hierarchies. You are encouraged to innovate through your own Gifts, and find the best way of working with this material. Contemplate your Gene Keys and their lines, and you will soon find a natural method emerging to suit your character and lifestyle. Contemplation remains an internal process, but it can also be powerful to share the insights of your contemplation at intervals with others.

In your relationships, as was mentioned earlier in the text, it is not always the case that your partner will want to use this material. If this is the case you needn't worry. The Venus Sequence only requires one person to shift the initial frequency of the relationship dynamic. As you break out of your victim patterns, of thinking, feeling, and reacting, your partner will naturally be invited into a greater awareness of their own patterns. Remember also not to be too rigid in following your own lines and Gene Keys. If you begin to see the patterns of other lines or Gene Keys outside your Profile, then use the wisdom of the Gene Keys to help you understand those other themes. Sometimes the mystery of life will not fit onto a single piece of paper!

You can also pay attention to the various dynamics that occur as different Shadow/Wound patterns engage with each other. For example, the dynamic of guilt as it interacts with repression is very different from the dynamic of guilt as it interacts with rejection.

It can be very illuminating to unpick the weave of the Shadow frequencies and the control we give them over our lives. Above all, this work needs time and patience. Awareness of the pattern is the greatest healing tool you have at your disposal. If you can see yourself behaving in a certain way, even though you may not like it, you are already half-way home. The unwinding of the wound only needs more time.

THE LOGARITHMIC HEALING OF 7-YEAR CYCLES

Time operates in a fractal pattern. This is one of the deepest insights of the whole Gene Keys transmission. Everything has its Divine timing. You have seen in this journey through your Venus Sequence how certain wound patterns are locked into your physical and subtle bodies at certain junctures in earlier cycles of your life. These moments of imprinting resurface as temporal portals throughout our lives. For example, if during your second 7-year cycle your parents divorced when you were 9 years old on August 12, then 7 years later on that very date, the same pattern will re-ignite in your DNA. Our physical cells are a living field of coded memories. In another 7 years the cycle will resurface yet again, and so on. How a pattern will reemerge is not known, but it will most likely come as some kind of a shock. If it was in your 1st 7-year physical cycle, the shock may be through your body. If it was in your 2nd 7-year cycle, it may be an emotional trauma and so on.

Our lives are therefore marked with opportunities. We do not need to know the dates of when certain themes will occur. Most of these events occurred too early in our lives for us to even remember them mentally, and as we have seen, they were all imprinted when we were in the womb in any case. The important insight to grasp is that times of challenge and difficulty are opportunities for deep healing. As your awareness enters more deeply into a pattern, you begin to reset the clock. You unwind the wound. All healing is logarithmic in this way. Working with the Venus Sequence, it will take you a full seven year cycle to penetrate the depth of any pre-birth pattern.

By the same token, you may find that after 9 months of working with this wisdom, you experience your first major breakthrough.

We do not know the twists and turns our healing journey will take in life. All we know is that there is a pattern, and once we have engaged our awareness of the Shadows, then that pattern will continue to unfold before our eyes. The healing process can be surprising, shattering, wondrous, magical, and probably the hardest thing you will ever undertake. The rewards of course are incalculable.

INTEGRATING THE VENUS SEQUENCE IN YOUR LIFE AND RELATIONSHIPS

Over the years I have been asked to try and simplify the transmission of the Gene Keys, so that it might become palatable and understandable for a mass market. Despite my best attempts, the Gene Keys continue to emerge in the language of my own culture and conditioning and through the language of my own Gene Keys and their lines. The Venus Sequence in particular requires a profound understanding before it ought to be shared in a therapeutic context. It is always tempting to take a new knowledge out into the world before it is fully embodied inside us. Having said that, this is sometimes a part of our healing process.

The Gene Keys Synthesis is a living transmission of wisdom and awareness. It is designed to be propagated by people who feel its truth resonating within their own DNA. The process of Self Illumination also comes through deep patience. It comes unexpectedly, and is conveyed mysteriously through the tone of your voice, the light in your eyes, the lightness of your touch. I ask that each of you who is reading this give yourself time to digest it. If you wish to help another then feel free to offer them guidance if they are receptive, but also direct them to this program. If you have gained insight through your own commitment and self-awareness, then it makes sense to encourage others to also use the same path.

We live in a time in which many spiritual teachings are coming out into the world. Many of them supply answers through techniques, or teachers that may be inspiring but do all the work for us. In this sense there is nothing more powerful than contemplation. You are a mystery and the Gene Keys Golden Path provides you with a route into your mystery, but the travelling is all up to you. You must put in the work. You must knock on the doors. The Venus Sequence is a profound wisdom that may require the rest of your life to really get to grips with. This is a spiritual path in its own right, so you can draw sustenance from that perspective. You can settle down into the wonderful freedom that deep contemplation affords you.

GOLDEN RULES FOR THE GOLDEN PATH - A NEW VISION OF RELATIONSHIPS

The Venus Sequence is primarily a transformational tool that uses our relationships as a spiritual path for our own awakening. As you learn to be compassionate towards yourself, cradling yourself in the lap of self-love, you may find that a whole new vision of relationships begins to emerge before your eyes.

Most of us have inherited a romantic view of relationships - that they must be passionate, empowering, and 'perfect'. These are certainly understandable desires to have, but the truth is that every relationship is unique and is defined by its chemistry and karma. Every relationship in your life is a spiritual journey in the sense that it will test you and teach you and stretch you in some way.

Once you begin working with your own Venus Sequence, you may find that your inner definition of a 'perfect relationship' begins to loosen. There is something of beauty in every relationship if you can just see and accept its limitations. We will do well to remember the first golden rule of the Golden Path:

1. Frequency is translated into chemistry.

The vibratory pitch of your attitude at any given moment is transferred to your DNA and quickly becomes your reality. Knowing this you have the freedom to choose how you design your life.

It is you who designs your own health, your own relationships, and your own inner fulfilment.

The second golden rule comes in the form of another caution; that we need to be very careful about using our knowledge (consciously or unconsciously) as a weapon. In our relationships we can all too easily point out the Shadows of others. Our ego can get a hold of knowledge and use it to try and help someone else, when in fact your urge to help the other has become a distraction from your own process. If you wish to truly help others, then you would do best to forget their Shadows altogether and contemplate their Gifts and Siddhis. If they are caught in a Shadow pattern then give them the frequency of their Siddhi as a response. Model the higher frequencies of others for others. The Shadows are for you alone!

Let this therefore be the second golden rule for the Golden Path:

2. With yourself, increase awareness of your Shadows. With others, increase awareness of their Gifts and Siddhis.

The 2nd golden rule also brings a reminder of the 3rd, which is that you must also increase your awareness of your own Gifts and Siddhis, as this will enable you to look upon your own Shadows with a kindly and forgiving eye. This involves the use of your imagination. Our imagination is magical because it has the capacity to open up our astral body, our emotions. Think of a film or book or poem that catches your imagination and opens up the heart suddenly. With the Gene Keys, we imagine ourselves into those Siddhis. We begin to allow ourselves to become a Buddha, a Christ, a saint. We open our mind and heart up to the limitless possibilities of life. And then our Core Purpose begins to activate. This whole stream of pathways through the Activation and Venus Sequence – begins to open up and expand our consciousness. This is the purpose of our contemplative inquiry. Through a systematic, sequential use of our imagination, we gradually begin to imbibe the central truths of the Gene Keys. We begin to resonate with the holographic language, and we see and feel its logic working inside us.

The 3rd Golden rule therefore concerns the use of our imagination:

3. Use the limitless power of your imagination to create a new and ever-expanding attitude to your life and your relationships.

A FINAL GIFT

The deepest truths are always the simplest. One final gift comes in the form of a simple and practical tip for both men and women that can immediately improve the dynamic of your primary relationship. This is something you can pass on to anyone in your life and watch the beginning of a transformation in their relationship.

Women: You are the heart and hearth of the relationship. Since time immemorial male DNA has needed to go out into the world and hunt. This means that the man has a profound archetypal need to go out the door and return. More than anything the male psyche relaxes when he knows he can leave freely and return to a welcoming embrace. This is a feeling to recreate at whatever level your imagination and lifestyle dictates. Let him feel both free and welcome in a way that feels balanced and fair to you.

Men: Let your woman know that she is at the centre of your life. Wherever you are and whatever you are involved in, whether she is present or not, consider her feelings. You do not necessarily need to share this, because she will feel it intuitively. If your woman feels that there is anything more important to you than your relationship with her, she will no longer feel safe or relaxed in the relationship. Give her the gift of your absolute commitment.

CONCLUSION TO THE VENUS SEQUENCE - OPENING INTO SYNARCHY

In the Golden Path, your Venus Sequence provides the greatest inner work. It is the heart of this transmission. You can see that it sits between the Activation Sequence and the Pearl Sequence, between purpose and prosperity. Before even attempting to transmute the karma of your relationships, you need to feel some sense of alignment to your higher purpose.

You need to develop a certain level of inner Core Stability. Your Venus Sequence will continually test and strengthen your Core Stability as you dive deeper into it. At the same time, your relationship will also continually bring you into alignment with your higher purpose, making your Life's Work clearer to you.

Your Venus Sequence will in turn engage the higher components of your Pearl Sequence. The Pearl concerns the awakening of a higher collective intelligence that moves across entire gene pools. It is a phenomenon known as Synarchy. Described in the 44th Siddhi, Synarchy is a mysterious self-organising principle that lies in wait in humanity's collective DNA. As we awaken through our relationships and open up our hearts, so our higher purpose begins to move us into fractal groupings in order to maximise efficiency and catalyse a global awakening through the pooling of our resources. This process is described in depth through the Pearl Sequence, which brings the Venus Sequence onto a much broader field of play.

As you engage your personal awakening through the Venus Sequence, you may well find that you wish to share this wisdom and have ideas and impulses to work with it in more depth in the world. It is a good idea to give yourself plenty of digestion time with the Venus Sequence before you therefore move onto the insights of the Pearl. I recommend you have a pause in between each of the Sequences of the Golden Path. It is always a good idea to put the knowledge down and do something else for a while, just to let it settle and stew inside your being. Give yourself a pat on the back and take a holiday. The Synarchy is coming!

14. RELEVANT TERMINOLOGY FOR CONTEMPLATION

Now you have read this whole book you have digested some extraordinary truths. By now you may be more accustomed to the language of the Gene Keys. However, the depth of the material you are currently digesting can be greatly enhanced and integrated inside you by further contemplation of the terminology that has been used. The following terms are all relevant to your journey through the Venus Sequence. The Gene Keys language is highly specific and is designed to literally communicate with the DNA in your body. Therefore reading these terms can be a transformational experience in itself. Give yourself some time to contemplate them - sit back, put on some music and allow them to percolate your consciousness!

Absorption — A state of consciousness in which your aura begins to feed off its own light, thus perpetuating a very stable high frequency throughout your being. As you enter the state of Absorption, your DNA begins to trigger your endocrine system to secrete certain rarefied hormones on a continual basis. These hormones are associated with higher brain functioning, and involve states of spiritual illumination and transcendence. At such a stage, it is no longer possible for you to be drawn back into the lower frequencies for more than brief periods of time. Arising naturally out of Contemplation and leading to Embodiment, Absorption occurs when you first begin to inhabit the buddhic body, after the Fourth Initiation.

Astral Body — The 2nd major subtle layer of your aura, corresponding to the astral plane. Of all the subtle bodies, the astral body is closest in vibration to the physical body and its etheric counterpart, which means that your emotional life has the most powerful and direct effect on your physical health and vitality.

The astral body is gradually developed in your 2nd seven-year cycle, from the age of 8 until 14, during which time all your major emotional patterns are laid down.

As you contemplate the Shadow consciousness field and how it affects and governs you personally, you are reaching down into your astral body and re-imprinting your basic emotional patterns with a higher frequency. This will bring about a major transformation in all your relationships, as you become less reactive and more emotionally mature.

Astral Plane — The 2nd of the 7 major planes of reality upon which all human beings function. The astral plane is a subtle electromagnetic field generated by all low frequency human desire and emotion. On the astral plane of reality, your every feeling or desire has an independent existence, and can be understood as an entity with its own vibratory frequency. Through the law of affinity, you draw into your aura the astral entities that match the frequency of your feelings and desires.

As you purify your emotional nature, it gradually becomes impossible for astral entities to influence your life and feelings. At this point you begin to function on the higher octave of the astral plane, known as the buddhic plane.

Atmic Body — The 6th major subtle layer of your aura, corresponding to the atmic plane and the Christ consciousness. Your atmic body, which manifests through the 64 Siddhis, is so vast that it defies comprehension. To enter fully into this body, your identification with the lower bodies — physical, emotional (astral), and mental must be severed completely. When this happens, your cycle of incarnations will come to an end. The atmic body creates an increasing pressure on your lower nature as its light gradually filters down to illuminate the lower three bodies, resulting in a magnificent phenomenon known as the dawning of the rainbow body. Over time, this leads to a complete restructuring of your life as the inner light of the Atmic plane dawns inside you, culminating in your full embodiment of divinity.

Atmic Plane — The 6th of the 7 major planes of reality upon which all human beings function. The atmic plane is the higher frequency octave of the mental plane, and is the plane of your true 'higher self'. On the atmic plane of reality, the entire cosmos is experienced as a living mind whose primary impulse is love.

When you cross the threshold to this plane (through the Sixth Initiation), then all your independent thinking immediately ceases — to be replaced by pure light. To contact your greater being on the atmic plane, all you have to do is focus consistently and intently on this inner light.

Contemplation — One of the three primary paths leading to the higher states of Absorption and Embodiment. Contemplation is the central path, represented by the Tao. It utilises elements of both Concentration (effort) and Meditation (no effort) to bring about a heightening of your frequency. Contemplation takes place on all three of the lower human planes; there is physical contemplation, emotional contemplation, and mental contemplation. Over time, contemplation transforms the physical, astral, and mental bodies into their higher frequency counterparts — the causal, buddhic, and atmic bodies.

Prolonged Contemplation on the 64 Gene Keys is one of the quickest and easiest ways to activate the higher frequencies lying latent within your DNA.

Corpus Christi – One of the twelve journeys making up the Gene Keys Synthesis, the Corpus Christi is the complete science of the 'Rainbow Body' – the true underlying nature of all human beings. The Corpus Christi is a synthesis of transmissions, teachings, and techniques that underpins the 64 Gene Keys. Representing the higher 'Mystery School' teachings of the Gene Keys, it includes the teaching of the Seven Seals, the Seven Sacred Bodies, and the Nine Initiations. Deep immersion in the teachings of the Corpus Christi assists you in grounding and embodying the higher frequencies of light into your everyday life. These are the teachings and techniques that allow you to draw the transmission of the Gene Keys layer by layer into the subtle bodies that make up your aura. Literally meaning 'The Body of Christ', the Corpus Christi prepares you to work with higher evolutionary frequencies by progressively purifying the many dimensions of your inner being, beginning with your physical body.

Embodiment — The natural culmination of the process of Concentration, Meditation, or Contemplation. After you attain the state of Absorption (the Fourth and Fifth Initiations), you eventually make the great quantum leap into full Embodiment (the Sixth Initiation). Embodiment relates to what many traditions know as enlightenment or realisation. It involves the complete embodiment of the higher three bodies onto their corresponding lower planes. The process of embodiment begins from the moment you are born into a human body, and it follows the trajectory of your evolution. The more evolved you are, the more embodied you become.

Evolution — An impetus or higher 'will' innate in all material forms. The current of evolution is responsible for gradually raising the vibratory frequency of all matter, even matter without awareness. As forms evolve, they gradually assume awareness, and in time transcend their sense of separation and return to their formless essence.

There are many spheres of evolution, all interconnected with each other, and human evolution is but one. Evolution represents that force within matter that always strives upwards towards spirit, as opposed to involution, its counter-force, which is the essence of spirit descending or embedding itself within the form.

Fractal — The holographic manifestation of light as it enters the material world and illuminates its true nature. A fractal is an endlessly repeating natural pattern that is maintained throughout the universe regardless of scale. For instance, the microscopic patterns within the membranes of cells in the human body are similar to those observed across the landscape of the earth when viewed from space. Similarly, the geometric laws that govern galactic nebulae are visually replicated when you slice a fruit in half. The more deeply you realise the fractal nature of reality, the more embodied and loving you become.

Every act you make in life generates a fractal wave pattern that affects all creatures in the universe. Through a process of continual evolutionary biofeedback, you can refine your life to such a point that you are in complete resonance with every fractal aspect of the universe.

Fractal Line — When our current universe was conceived at the moment of the Big Bang, the crystalline seed of our evolution shattered into countless fractal shards or fragments. These fractal aspects of the whole radiated out in precise geometric patterns known as fractal lines. All fractal lines can be traced back to one of three primary fractal lines, thus seeding the trinity within all aspects of the holographic universe. As you move into deeper harmony with your true nature, you come into alignment with all beings within your seed fractal line, which catalyses great synchronicity and grace in your life.

Involution — The means by which Grace — that Divine essence that lies beyond all understanding — incarnates progressively into form. Involution is the counter-force to Evolution — that current which gives us the impression we are progressing and evolving of our own accord. From the point of view of involution, all things are predestined and there can be no individual free will, since all events are simply playing themselves out according to a higher unraveling. As evolution evokes aspiration towards something higher, so involution invokes inspiration as something higher that already lies inside us waiting to be discovered.

Karma — Karma refers to the specific slice of suffering you have undertaken to transform during your lifetime. The agents of karma are your sanskaras — the specific manifestations of karma as it is played out in your life. From the point of view of the Gene Keys Synthesis, karma is understood in a different way from its traditional form. For instance, karma cannot be personal, but is always a collective phenomenon. This means that all acts are performed by the whole, for the purpose of the whole. Neither does karma carry retribution or reward beyond our lifetime. However, in the bardo state beyond death, we come face to face with our karma in a form so powerful it cannot be described. Therefore it is always in our interest to take full responsibility for our actions during our lifetime. Karma is determined according to the level of frequency made manifest in our subtle bodies, and by the stage we have reached as we move through the Nine Initiations (described in the 22nd Gene Key).

Mental Body — The mental body exists at a higher frequency than your emotions, and is constructed out of your thinking life. The mental body is greatly influenced by the collective mental body of humanity itself, which tends to pull our thinking down into the unfulfilled desires of the astral body. As your thinking revolves around higher impulses, the mental body gradually disentangles itself from the astral body and takes on greater power. The mental body can also be used by the lower consciousness to repress the natural impulses of the astral body, which can also lead to problems in health at all levels. A low frequency and limiting mental paradigm sets up low frequency emotional patterns within the astral body, whereas a high frequency mental paradigm creates emotional clarity and freedom.

Mental Plane — The 3rd of the 7 major planes of reality upon which all human beings function. The mental plane is the frequency plane created and dominated by the energy of thought. On the mental plane, all thoughts and ideas have an independent life that human beings either attract or repel. The mental plane itself is made up of different strata of mental energies that resonate at different frequencies. A low frequency mental paradigm for example, is created by thought patterns that are self-limiting, creating division and separation. Such a paradigm activates neural pathways that are based upon fear and survival. A high frequency mental paradigm is characterised by a mental openness that encourages insight and breakthrough from the higher causal plane. This kind of thinking is unifying, positive, and sees where things are interconnected, rather than where they are threatened. As you enter a higher mode of thinking based on how to be of greater service to others and to the whole, all manner of insights and gifts begin to dawn in your mind. Eventually, your awareness transcends the frequencies of thought altogether, and you rise above the mental plane and experience true clarity.

Sanskaras — Biogenetic memories that are passed down all ancestral lines. Your sanskaras are the 'wound opportunities' that you have inherited during your lifetime. Such memories are more than simple memories held in the mind, but are charges of kinetic energy that give rise to your behavioural patterns, beliefs, and general outlook. Sanskaras are not in any way personal, nor are they the result of actions in past lives. Rather, your sanskaras determine the specific themes of the great challenges you will face during your life. Once you realise that such patterns are not caused consciously by you, but are your greatest opportunities for transformation and evolution, the challenges in your life become much easier to bear. The Venus Sequence provides a systematic means of tracking and transforming the specific sanskaras that you carry during your lifetime.

Transmission — A higher field of consciousness whose sole purpose is to penetrate and awaken those aspects of itself that still remain unaware of their greater reality. Most transmissions assume the form of a teaching or set of teachings that enter the world exactly when the world is ready to receive them. All transmissions follow natural 'fractal lines' as they spread throughout humanity, bringing with them a higher order of consciousness. Even though transmissions may take the form of words and practices, their true nature lies shrouded in mystery. The Gene Keys Transmission is a part of the wave of awakening, generated as the Great Change is felt in the world.

Transmutation — The process of dynamic and permanent change that comes about as you surrender and accept mutation. At the Shadow frequency, mutation is something that is greatly feared as it always challenges an established pattern, rhythm, or routine. Unless mutations (periods of natural upheaval) are embraced and fully accepted in your life, transmutation cannot occur.

Transmutation involves a complete shift from one state or plane to another. After a transmutation, nothing is ever the same again. Transmutation only begins to occur at the Gift frequency band, as your deepest cellular victim patterns are transformed through awareness. Periods of intense mutation in your life are always a great opportunity for transmutation. So long as your attitude is open-hearted and accepting, and you embrace and take responsibility for your own state, transmutation will occur in your life. With transmutation come great clarity, freedom, and creativity. It is the process through which your genius emerges into the world.

Trinity — The underlying nature of all manifest form. As form emerges from the undivided state of the formless, it spontaneously moves from one to three. To the human mind and our current perception, it appears that all around us is a binary. Because of the limitations of our current awareness, the trinity at the heart of creation is not easily apparent. The trinity is the reflection of the infinite, whereas the binary is the reflection of the finite. As you raise the frequency of your DNA and begin to see through a higher kind of vision, one of the first patterns you will recognise is the trinity. As the fundamental building block of the holographic universe, the pattern of the trinity allows life to keep on transcending and evolving. It ensures that nothing can ever be consistent and fixed, even though things may appear so. As you begin to attune your mind and heart to the secret nature of the trinity, you will begin to relax more and more deeply into the Truth of the inherent self-ordering perfection of the universe.

THE GENE KEYS GOLDEN PATH

PROSPERITY

A Guide To Your Venus Sequence

A PERSONAL INVITATION FROM RICHARD RUDD

Congratulations! It takes a valiant soul to persevere the whole way through one's Venus Sequence. This amazing work will continue to ripen in your life and open up new possibilities in your relationships. You have chosen the most fruitful and potent spiritual path in existence - the path of love. As your awareness continues to open up your heart, it will pick up its own delicious momentum until your opening takes on a life of its own.

This rewarding inner transformation naturally carries an urge to now share your heart in a far wider way in the world. Love engenders synchronicity and that brings about a new level of prosperity. This deeper opening to a wider collective field is described and further refined in your Pearl Sequence, the grand finale in your Golden Path journey. The Pearl is your harvest, bringing grace and fortune back into your life on levels you may not have dreamed of since you were a child.

I encourage you therefore to take the final step into your Pearl Sequence, when you feel ready, and complete your epic voyage into the myriad mysteries of your innermost being.

I wish you love and blessings on your continuing journey…

Richard Rudd

CPSIA information can be obtained
at www.ICGtesting.com
Printed in the USA
LVHW070320020921
696644LV00013B/43

9 781999 671013